Jean-Jacques Rousseau

A Treatise on the Social Compact or the Principles of Politic Law

Jean-Jacques Rousseau

A Treatise on the Social Compact or the Principles of Politic Law

ISBN/EAN: 9783337069438

Printed in Europe, USA, Canada, Australia, Japan

Cover: Foto ©Suzi / pixelio.de

More available books at **www.hansebooks.com**

TREATISE

ON THE

SOCIAL COMPACT;

OR

The PRINCIPLES of

POLITIC LAW.

By J. J. ROUSSEAU,

Citizen of GENEVA.

A NEW EDITION.

——————— Fœderis æquas
Dicamus leges.   Æneid. xi.

LONDON:

Printed for J. MURRAY, N° 32, Fleet-Street.

M DCC XCI.

ADVERTISEMENT.

THIS little treatife is taken from a much larger work, in which I formerly engaged, without having duly confulted my abilities. I have, therefore, long fince laid it afide; conceiving it proper to offer the following extract only to the public, as the leaft extionable part of the performance.

CONTENTS.

BOOK I.

In which the transition from a state of nature to that of society, is investigated, with the essential conditions of the social compact.

CHAP.

CONTENTS.

CHAP. IV.

BOOK

CONTENTS.

BOOK II.

Concerning the Legiſlature.

CHAP.

CONTENTS.

BOOK III.

Concerning political laws, or the forms of Government.

CHAP.

CONTENTS.

CHAP. II.

CHAP. III.

CHAP. IV.

CHAP. V.

CHAP. VI.

CHAP VII.

CHAP. VIII.

CHAP.

C O N T E N T S.

C H A P. IX.

C H A P. X.

C H A P. XI.

C H A P. XII.

C H A P. XIII.

C H A P. XIV.

C H A P. XV.

C H A P.

CONTENTS.

CHAP. XVI.

CHAP. XVII.

CHAP. XVIII.

BOOK IV.

In which the ſubject of political laws is continued, and the means of ſtrengthening the conſtitution of the ſtate conſidered.

CHAP. I.

CHAP. II.

CHAP.

CONTENTS.

A

A

T R E A T I S E

ON THE

SOCIAL COMPACT, &c.

BOOK I.

INTRODUCTION.

MY defign, in the prefent treatife, is to inquire, Whether the nature of fociety admits of any fixed and equitable rules of government, fuppofing mankind to be fuch as they are, and their laws fuch as they might be made. In this inveftigation I fhall endeavour conftantly to join the confiderations of natural right and public intereft, fo that juftice and utility may never be difunited.

This being premifed, I fhall enter on my fubject, without expatiating on its importance. If

B   it

it be afked, Whether I am a prince or legiflator, that I thus take upon me to write on politics? I anfwer, I am neither ; and that it is for
this reafon I write.   Were I a prince or legiflator I would not throw away my time in pointing
out what ought to be done ; I would myfelf put
it in practice, or be filent.

As the citizen of a free ftate, and a member
of the fupreme power, by birth, however weak
may be the influence of my fingle vote in public
affairs, the right of giving that vote is fufficient
to impofe on me the duty of making thofe affairs
my ftudy, thinking myfelf happy in difcuffing the
various forms of government, to find every day
new reafons for admiring that of my own country * !

CHAP. I.

The fubject of the firft book.

MAN is born free, and yet is univerfally
enflaved.   At the fame time, an individual frequently conceives himfelf to be the lord
and mafter over others, though only more emi-
nently deprived of liberty.   Whence can this
change arife ? Are there any means by which
it may be rendered lawful ? The former quef-

* Geneva.

tion

tion I cannot anfwer, though I imagine myfelf capable of refolving the latter.

If I took into confideration only the exiftence and effects of power, I fhould fay, So long as a people are compelled to obey, they do well to be obedient ; but, as foon as they are in a capacity to refift, they do better to throw off the yoke of reftraint : For, in recovering their liberty on the fame plea by which they loft it, either they have a juft right to reaffume it, or thofe could have none who deprived them of it. But there is an inviolable right founded on the very nature of fociety, which ferves as the bafis of all others. Man doth not derive this right, however, immediately from nature; it is founded on mutual convention. We muft proceed, then, to inquire, of what kind fuch convention muft have been. But, before we come to argue this point, I fhould eftablifh what I have already advanced.

C H A P. II.

On the primitive ftate of fociety.

THE moft ancient of all focieties, and the only natural one, is that of a family. And even in this, children are no longer connected with their father, than while they ftand in need of his affiftance. When this becomes

needlefs,

needlefs, the natural tie is of courfe diffolved, the children are exempted from the obedience they owe their father, and the father is equally fo from the folicitude due from him to his children ; both affume a ftate of independence refpecting each other. They may continue, indeed, to live together afterwards ; but their connection, in fuch a cafe, is no longer natural, but voluntary; and even the family union is then maintained by mutual convention.

This liberty, which is common to all man-kind, is the neceffary confequence of our very nature; whofe firft law being that of felf-pre-fervation, our principal concerns are thofe which relate to ourfelves; no fooner, therefore, doth man arrive at years of difcretion, than he be-comes the only proper judge of the means of that prefervation, and of courfe his own mafter.

In a family, then, we may fee the firft model of political focieties : their chief is reprefented by the father, and the people by his children, while all of them being free, and equal by birth, they cannot alienate their liberty, but for their common intereft. All the difference between a fa-mily and a ftate, lies in this, That, in the former, the love which a father naturally bears to his children is a compenfation for his folicitude con-cerning them ; and, in the latter, it is the pleafure

of

of command that supplies the place of this love, which a chief doth not entertain for his people.

Grotius denies that government is invested with power solely for the benefit of those who are governed, and cites the case of slaves as an example. It is, indeed, his constant practice, to establish the matter of right on the matter of fact *. He might have employed a more conclusive method, though not a more favourable one for tyrannical governments.

It is then doubtful, according to Grotius, whether the whole race of mankind, except about an hundred individuals, belong to those individuals, or whether the latter belong to the whole race of mankind; and he appears, throughout his whole work, to lean to the former opinion. This is also the opinion of Hobbes. Thus they divide the human species into herds of cattle, each of which hath its keeper, who protects it from others, only that he may make a property of it himself.

* " The learned researches into the laws of nature and nations are often nothing more than the history of ancient abuses; so that it is a ridiculous infatuation to be too fond of studying them." *Manuscript Treatise on the Interests of France, by the Marquis d'A.* This was exactly the case with Grotius.

B 3

As

As a shepherd is of a superior nature to his flock, so the herd-keepers of men, or their chiefs, are of a superior nature to the herd, over which they preside. Such was the reasoning, according to Philo, of the Emperor Caligula, who concluded logically enough from this analogy, that either kings were gods, or their subjects no better than brutes.

This argument of Caligula bears much resemblance to those of Hobbes and Grotius. Aristotle had said, indeed, before either of them, that men were not naturally equal; but that some of them were born to slavery, and others to dominion.

Aristotle was right as to the fact, but mistook the effect for the cause. Nothing is more certain, than that every man born in slavery is born to be a slave. In such a state, men lose even the desire of freedom, and prefer subjection, as the companions of Ulysses did their brutality *. If there are any slaves, therefore, by nature, it is because they are slaves contrary to nature. Power first made slaves, and cowardice hath perpetuated them.

* See a little tract written by Plutarch, on the rationality of brutes.

I have

I have said nothing of king Adam, or the emperor Noah, father of three monarchs, who, like the children of Saturn, as some have imagined them to be, divided the world among them. I hope my moderation also in this respect will be esteemed some merit; for, as I am descended in a right line from one of these princes, and probably from the eldest branch of the family, how do I know, that, by a regular deduction of my descent, I might not find myself the legitimate heir to universal monarchy? Be this, however, as it may, it cannot be denied, that Adam had as good a title to the sovereignty of the world, when he was the only person in it, as Robinson Crusoe had to that of his island under the same circumstances. A very great conveniency also attended their government, in that the monarch might rest securely on his throne, without fear of wars, conspiracies, or rebellion.

C H A P. III.

On the right of the Strongest.

THE strongest is not strong enough to continue always master, unless he transforms his power into a right of command, and obedience into a duty. Hence is deduced the right of the strongest; a right taken ironically in ap-

pearance,

pearance, and laid down as an established principle in reality. But will this term never be
rightly explained? Force, in the simplest sense,
is a physical power; nor can I see what morality
can result from its effects. To yield to superior
force is an act of necessity, not of the will; at
most it is but an act of prudence. And in what
sense can this be called a duty?

Let us suppose, however, for a moment, this
pretended right established, and we shall see it
attended with inexplicable absurdities; for, if it
be admitted, that power constitutes right, the
effect changes with the cause, and every succeed-
ing power, if greater than 'the former, succeeds
also to the right; so that men may lawfully dif-
obey, as soon as they can do it, with impunity;
and, as right is always on the strongest side,
they have nothing more to do, than to acquire
superior force. Now what kind of right can
that be, which vanishes with the power of en-
forcing it? If obedience be only exacted by com-
pulsion, there is no need to make such obedience
a duty, as when we are no longer compelled to
obey, we are no longer obliged to it. It appears, therefore, that the word *right* adds nothing in this case to that of force, and, in fact,
is a term of no signification.

Be obedient to the higher powers. If by this precept is meant, *fubj·ct to a fuperior force,* the advice is good, though fuperfluous; I will anfwer for it, fuch a rule will never be broken. All power, I own, is derived from God; but every corporeal malady is derived alfo from the fame fource. But are we therefore forbid to call in the phyfician? If a robber fhould ftop me on the highway, am I not only obliged, on compulfion, to give him my purfe, but am I alfo obliged to it in point of confcience, though I might poffibly conceal it from him? This will hardly be averred; and yet the piftol he holds to my breaft, is, in effect, a fuperior force.

On the whole, we muft conclude, then, that mere power doth not conftitute right, and that men are obliged only to pay obedience to lawful authority. Thus we are conftantly recurring to my firft queftion.

CHAP. IV.

On flavery.

AS no man hath any natural authority over the reft of his fpecies, and as power doth not confer right, the bafis of all lawful authority is laid in mutual convention.

If an individual, fays Grotius, can alienate his liberty, and become the flave of a mafter, why may not a whole people collectively alienate theirs, and become fubject to a king? This propofition, however, contains fome equivocal terms, which require explanation, but I fhall confine myfelf to that of *alienate*. Whatever is alienated muft be difpofed of, either by gift or fale. Now a man who becomes the flave of another doth not give himfelf away, but fells himfelf, at leaft for his fubfiftence; but why fhould a whole people fell themfelves? So far is a king from furnifhing his fubjects fubfiftence, that they maintain him; and, as our friend Rabelais fays, A king doth not live on a little. Can fubjects be fuppofed to give away their liberty, on condition that the receiver fhall take their property along with it? After this, I really cannot fee any thing they have left.

It may be faid, a monarch maintains among his fubjects the public tranquillity. Be it fo; I would be glad to know, of what they are gainers, if the wars in which his ambition engages them, if his infatiable avarice, or the oppreffions of his minifters, are more deftructive than civil diffenfions? Of what are they gainers, if even this tranquillity be one caufe of their mifery? A prifoner may live tranquil enough in his dungeon; but will this be fufficient to make him contented there? When the Greeks were fhut

up

up in the cave of the Cyclops, they lived there unmolefted, in expectation of their turn to be devoured.

To fay, that a man can give himfelf away, is to talk unintelligibly and abfurdly; fuch an act muft neceffarily be illegal and void, were it for no other reafon, than that it argues infanity of mind in the agent. To fay the fame thing of a whole people therefore, is to fuppofe a whole nation can be at once out of their fenfes; but were it fo, fuch madnefs could not confer right.

Were it poffible alfo for a man to alienate himfelf, he could not, in the fame manner, difpofe of his children, who, as human beings, are born free; their freedom is their own, and no-body hath any right to difpofe of it but them-felves. Before they arrive at years of difcretion, indeed, their father may, for their fecurity, and in their name, ftipulate the conditions of their prefervation, but he cannot unconditionally and irrevocably difpofe of their perfons, fuch a gift being contrary to the intention of nature, and exceeding the bounds of paternal authority. It is requifite, therefore, in order to render an ar-bitrary government lawful, that every new ge-neration fhould be at liberty to admit or reject its authority, in which cafe it would be no longer an arbitrary government.

To

To renounce one's natural liberty, is to renounce one's very being as a man; it is to renounce not only the rights, but even the duties
of humanity. And what poſſible indemnification
can be made the man who thus gives up his all?
Such a renunciation is incompatible with our
very nature; for to deprive us of the liberty of
the will, is to take away all morality from our
actions. In a word, a convention, which ſtipu-
lates on the one part abſolute authority, and on
the other implicit obedience, is, in itſelf, futile and contradictory. Is it not evident, that
we can lie under no reciprocal obligation whatever to a perſon, of whom we have a right to
demand every thing; and doth not this circum-
ſtance, againſt which he has no equivalent, neceſſarily infer ſuch act of convention to be void?
For what claim can my ſlave have upon me,
when he himſelf, and all that belongs to him,
are mine? His claims are of courſe my own, and
to ſay thoſe can be ſet up againſt me, is to talk
abſurdly.

Again, Grotius and others have deduced the
origin of this pretended right from the ſuperiority
obtained in war. The conqueror, ſay they, having a right to put the vanquiſhed to death, the
latter may equitably purchaſe his life at the expence of his liberty; ſuch an agreement being

9   the

the more lawful, as it conduces to the mutual advantage of both parties.

It is clear and certain, however, that this pretended right of the victor over the lives of the vanquished is not, in any shape, the natural result of a state of war. This is plain, were it for no other reason than that the reciprocal relations of mankind, while living together in their primitive independence, were not sufficiently durable, to constitute a state, either of peace or war; so that men cannot be naturally enemies. It is the relation subsisting between things, and not between men, that gives rise to war; which arising thus, not from personal, but real, relations, cannot subsist between man and man, either in a state of nature, in which there is no settled property, or in a state of society, in which every thing is secured by the laws.

The quarrels, encounters and duels of individuals are not sufficient to constitute such a state of war; and, with regard to the particular combats authorised by the institutions of Lewis XI. King of France; they were only some of the abuses of the feudal government, a system truly absurd, as contrary to the principles of natural justice, as of good policy.

War

War is not, therefore, any relation between man and man, but a relation between ſtate and ſtate, in which individuals are enemies only accidentally, not as men, or even as citizens, but as ſoldiers; not as members of their particular community, but as its defenders. In ſhort, a ſtate can have for its enemy nothing but a ſtate, not men ; as between things eſſentially different, there can be no common relation.

This principle is, indeed, conformable to the eſtabliſhed maxims of all ages, and the conſtant practice of every civilized people. Declarations of war are made leſs to give notice to ſovereigns, than to their ſubjects.

The foreigner, whether a ſovereign, an individual, or a people, who plunders, kills, or takes priſoner a ſubject, without declaring war againſt his prince, is not an enemy, but a robber. Even in a time of war, a juſt prince may make himſelf maſter, in an enemy's country, of whatever belongs to the public, but he will reſpect the perſons and private properties of individuals; he will reſpect thoſe rights on which his own are founded. The deſign of war being the deſtruction of an hoſtile ſtate, we have a right to kill its defenders, while they are in arms ; but as, in laying down their arms, they ceaſe to be enemies,

or

or inftruments of hoftility, they become, in that cafe, mere men, and we have not the leaft right to murder them. It is fometimes poffible effectually to deftroy a ftate, without killing even one of its members; now war cannot confer any right or privilege, which is not neceffary to accomplifh its end and defign. It is true, thefe are not the principles of Grotius, nor are they founded on the authority of the poets; but they are fuch as are deduced from the nature of things, and are founded on reafon.

With regard to the right of conqueft, it has no other foundation than that of force, the law of the ftrongeft. But, if war doth not give the victor a right to maffacre the vanquifhed, this pretended right, which does not exift, cannot be the foundation of a right to enflave them. If we have no right to kill an enemy, unlefs we cannot by force reduce him to flavery, our right to make him a flave never can be founded on our right to kill him. It is, therefore, an iniquitous bargain, to make him purchafe, at the expence of liberty, a life, which we have no right to take away. In eftablifhing thus a right of life and death over others, on that of enflaving them; and, on the other hand, a right of enflaving them on that of life and death, we certainly fall into the abfurdity of reafoning in a circle.

Let

Let us suppose, however, that this shocking right of general massacre existed, I still affirm, that a slave, made so by the fortune of war, or a conquered people, so reduced to slavery, lie under no other obligations to their master, than to obey him so long as he hath the power to compel them to it. In accepting of an equivalent for their lives, the victor confers on them no favour; instead of killing them uselessly, he hath only varied the mode of their destruction to his own advantage. So far, therefore, from his having acquired over them any additional authority, the state of war subsists between them as before; their relation to each other is the evident effect of it, and his exertion of the rights of war is a proof, that no treaty of peace hath succeeded. Will it be said, they have made a convention; be it so: This convention is a mere truce, and is so far from putting an end to the state of war, that it necessarily implies its continuation.

Thus, in whatever light we consider this affair, the right of making men slaves is null and void, not only because it is unjust, but because it is absurd and insignificant. The terms *slavery* and *justice* are contradictory and reciprocally exclusive of each other. Hence the following proposal

pofal would be equally ridiculous, whether
made by one individual to another, or by a private man to a whole people. *I enter into an
agreement with you, altogether at your own charge,
and folely for my profit, which I will obferve as
long as I pleafe, and which you are to obferve a'fo,
as long as I think proper.*

CHAP. V.

*On the neceſſity of recurring always to the primi-
tive convention.*

ON the fuppofition, that I fhould grant to
be true what I have hitherto difproved,
the advocate for defpotifm would, however,
profit but little. There will be always a great
difference between fubjecting a multitude, and
governing a fociety. Let individuals, in any
number whatever, become feverally and fuccef-
fively fubject to one man, they are all, in that
cafe, nothing more than mafter and flaves; they
are not a people governed by their chief; they
are an Aggregate if you will, but do not
form an affociation; there fubfift among them
neither commonwealth nor body politic. Such
a fuperior, though he fhould become the mafter
of half the world, would be ftill a private perfon, and his intereft, feparate and diftinct from
that of his people, would be ftill no more than a
private

private intereſt.   When ſuch a perſon dies, alſo
the empire over which he preſided is diſſolved,
and its component parts remain totally uncon-
nected, juſt as an oak falls into a heap of aſhes,
when it is conſumed by the fire.

A people, ſays Grotius, may voluntarily be-
ſtow themſelves on a king: According to Grotius, therefore, a people are a people before
they thus give themſelves up to regal authority.
Even this gift, however, is an act of ſociety, and
preſuppoſes a public deliberation on the matter.
Hence, before we examine into the act, by which
a people make choice of a king, it is proper to
examine into that by which a people became a
people, for, on this, which is neceſſarily prior
to the other, reſts the true foundation of ſociety.

For, if, in fact, there be no prior convention, whence ariſes (unleſs indeed the election
was unanimous) the obligation of the ſmaller
number to ſubmit to the choice of the greater?
and whence comes it, that an hundred perſons,
for inſtance, who might deſire to have a maſter,
had a right to vote for ten others who might deſire to have none? The choice by a plurality of
votes is in itſelf an eſtabliſhment of convention,
and ſuppoſes, that unanimity muſt at leaſt for
once have ſubſiſted among them.

CHAP.

CHAP. VI.

On the social pact or covenant.

I Suppofe mankind arrived at that term, when the obftacles to their prefervation, in a ftate of nature, prevail over the endeavours of individuals, to maintain themfelves in fuch a ftate. At fuch a crifis this primitive ftate therefore could no longer fubfift, and the human race muft have perifhed, if they had not changed their manner of living.

Now as men cannot create new powers, but only compound and direct thofe which really exift, they have no other means of prefervation; than that of forming, by their union, an accumulation of forces, fufficient to oppofe the obftacles to their fecurity, and of putting thefe in action by a firft mover, capable of making them act in concert with each other.

This general accumulation of power cannot arife but from the concurrence of many particular forces; but the force and liberty of each individual being the principal inftruments of his own prefervation, how is he to engage them in the common intereft, without hurting his own, and neglecting the obligations he lies under to himfelf ?

himſelf? This difficulty, being applied to my preſent ſubject, may be expreſſed in the following terms :

" To find that form of aſſociation which ſhall protect and defend, with the whole force of the community, the perſon and property of each individual, and in which each perſon, by uniting himſelf to the reſt, ſhall neverthelefs be obedient only to himſelf, and remain as fully at liberty as before." Such is the fundamental problem, of which the ſocial compact gives the ſolution.

The clauſes of this compact are ſo precifely determined by the nature of the act, that the leaſt reſtriction or modification renders them void and of no effect ; in ſo much, that, although they may perhaps never have been formally pro-mulgated, they are yet univerfally the ſame, and are every where tacitly acknowledged and received. When the ſocial pact, however, is violated, individuals recover their natural liberty, and are re-inveſted with their original rights, by loſing that conventional liberty for the fake of which they had renounced them.

Again ; theſe clauſes, well underſtood, are all reducible to one, *viz.* the total alienation of every individual, with all his rights and privileges,

leges, to the whole community. For, in the firft place, as every one gives himfelf up entirely and without referve, all are in the fame circumftances, fo that no one can be interefted in making their common connection burthenfome to others.

Befides, as the alienation is made without re-ferve, the union is as perfect as poffible, nor hath any particular affociate any thing to re-claim ; whereas, if they fhould feverally retain any peculiar privileges, there being no common um-pire to determine between them and the public, each being his own judge in fome cafes, would, in time, pretend to be fo in all, the ftate of na-ture would ftill fubfift, and their affociation would neceffarily become tyrannical or void.

In fine, the individual, by giving himfelf up to all, gives himfelf to none ; and, as he ac-quires the fame right over every other perfon in the community, as he gives them over himfelf, he gains an equivalent for what he beftows, and ftill a greater power to preferve what he retains.

If, therefore, we take from the focial compact every thing that is not effential to it, we fhall find it reduced to the following terms : " We, the contracting parties, do jointly and feverally fubmit our perfons and abilities, to the fupreme direction of the general will of all, and, in a
collective

collective body, receive each member into that body, as an indivisible part of the whole."

This act of association accordingly converts the several individual contracting parties into one moral collective body, composed of as many members as there are votes in the assembly, which receives also from the same act its unity and existence. This public personage, which is thus formed by the union of all its members, used formerly to be denominated a CITY *, and, at present,

* The true sense of this word is almost entirely perverted among the moderns; most people take a town for a city, and an house-keeper for a citizen. Such are ignorant, however, that, though houses may form a town, it is the citizens only that constitute a city. This same errour formerly cost the Carthaginians very dear. I do not remember, in the course of my reading, to have ever found the title of *Cives* given to the subjects of a prince, not even formerly to the Macedonians, nor, in our times, to the English, though more nearly bordering on liberty than any other nation. The French are the only people who familiarly take on themselves the name of *citizens*, because they have no just idea of its meaning, as may be seen in their dictionaries; for, were it otherwise, indeed, they would be guilty of high treason in assuming it. This term is with them rather expressive of a virtue than a privilege. Hence, when Bodin spoke of the citizens and inhabitants of Geneva,

prefent, takes the name of a *republic*, or *body politic*. It is alfo called, by its feveral members, a *ftate*, when it is paffive; the *fovereign*, when it is active; and fimply a *power*, when it is compared with other bodies of the fame nature. With regard to the affociates themfelves, they take collectively the name of the *people*, and are feparately called *citizens*, as partaking of the fovereign authority, and *fubjects*, as fubjected to the laws of the ftate. Thefe terms, indeed, are frequently confounded, and miftaken one for the other; it is fufficient, however, to be able to diftinguifh them, when they are to be ufed with precifion.

CHAP. VII.

Of the fovereign.

IT is plain from the above formula, that the act of affociation includes a reciprocal engagement between particulars and the public;

neva, he committed a wretched blunder, in miftaking one for the other. Mr. d'Alembert indeed has avoided this miftake in the Encyclopœdia, where he has properly diftinguifhed the four orders of people (and even five, reckoning mere ftrangers) that are found in our city, and of which two only compofe the republic: No other French author that I know of hath ever comprehended the meaning of the word *citizen*.

and

and that each individual, in contracting, if I may fo fay, with himfelf, is laid under a twofold engagement, *viz.* as a member of the fovereign-ty toward particular perfons, and as a member of the ftate toward the fovereign. That maxim of the civil law, however, is inapplicable here, which fays, that no one is bound by the engagements he enters into with himfelf; for there is a wide difference between entering into a perfonal obligation with one's felf, and with a whole, of which one may conftitute a part.

It is farther to be obferved, that the public determination, which is obligatory on the fub-ject, with regard to the fovereign, on account of the twofold relation by which each ftands con-tracted, is not, for the contrary reafon, obliga-tory on the fupreme power towards itfelf: and that it is confequently inconfiftent with the na-ture of the body politic, that fuch fupreme power fhould impofe a law, which it cannot break. For, as the fovereign ftands only in a fingle relation, it is in the fame cafe as that of an individual contracting with himfelf; whence it is plain, that there neither is, nor can be, any fundamental law obligatory on the whole body of a people, even the focial compact itfelf not being fuch. By this, however, it is not meant, that fuch a body cannot enter into engagements with others, in matters that do not derogate

from

from this contract; for, with refpect to foreign
objects, it is a fimple and individual perfon.

But, as the body politic, or the fovereign,
derives its very exiftence from this inviolable
contract, it can enter into no lawful engagement,
even with any fimilar body, derogatory from the
tenour of this primitive act; fuch as that of
alienating any part of itfelf, or of fubmitting itfelf intirely to a foreign fovereign. To violate
the act whereby it exifts would be to annihilate
itfelf, and from nothing can arife nothing.

No fooner are a multitude of individuals thus
united in a body, than it becomes impoffible to
act offenfively againft any of the members, without attacking the whole, and ftill lefs to offend
the whole body, without injuring the members.
Hence both duty and intereft equally oblige the
two contracting parties to affift each other, and
the fame perfons ought to endeavour to include,
within this twofold relation, all the advantages
which depend on it.

Now the fovereign, being formed only by
the feveral individuals of which the ftate is compofed, can have no intereft contrary to theirs; of
courfe the fupreme power ftands in no need of
any guarantee toward the fubjects, becaufe it is
C impoffible,

impoffible, that the body fhould be capable of
hurting all its members; and we fhall-fee hereafter, that it can as little tend to injure any of
them in particular.   Hence the fovereign is
neceffarily, and for the fame reafon that it exifts,
always fuch as it ought to be.

The cafe is different, however, as to the relation in which the fubjects ftand to the fovereign; as, notwithftanding their common intereft, the latter can have no fecurity that the
former will difcharge their engagements, unlefs
means be found to engage their fidelity.

In fact, every individual may, as a man, entertain a particular will, either contradictory or
diffimilar to his general will, as a citizen.   His
private intereft may influence him, in a manner
diametrically oppofite to the common intereft of
the fociety. Reflecting on his own exiftence as pofitive and naturally independent, he may conceive
what he owes to the common caufe, to be a free
and gratuitous contribution, the want of which
will be lefs hurtful to others, than the difcharge
of it will be burthenfome to himfelf; and, regarding the moral perfon of the ftate as an imaginary being, becaufe it is not a man, he may
be defirous of enjoying all the privileges of a
citizen, without fulfilling his engagement as a
                                                    fubject;

ſubject; an injuſtice, that, in its progreſs, muſt neceſſarily be the ruin of the body politic.

To the end, therefore, that the ſocial compact ſhould not prove an empty form, it tacitly includes this engagement, which only can enforce the reſt, *viz.* that whoſoever refuſes to pay obedience to the general will, ſhall be liable to be compelled to it by the force of the whole body. And this is in effect nothing more, than that they may be compelled to be free; for ſuch is the condition which, in uniting every citizen to the ſtate, ſecured him from all perſonal dependence; a condition, which forms the whole artifice and play of the political machine : it is this alone that renders all ſocial engagements juſt and equitable which, without it, would be abſurd, tyrannical, and ſubject to the moſt enormous abuſes.

CHAP. VIII.

Of civil ſociety in general.

THE tranſition of man from a ſtate of nature to a ſtate of ſociety is productive of a very remarkable change in his being, by ſubſtituting juſtice inſtead of inſtinct, as the rule of his conduct, and attaching that morality to his actions, of which they were before deſtitute. It is in immediate conſequence of this change, when

the

the voice of duty fucceeds to phyfical impulfe
and the law of appetite, that man, who hitherto
regarded only his own gratification, finds himfelf
obliged to act on other principles, and to con-
fult his reafon, before he follows the dictates of
his paffions. Although, by entering into a ftate
of fociety, he is deprived alfo of many advantages which depend on that of nature, he gains
by it others fo very confiderable, his faculties
exert and expand themfelves, his ideas arc en-
larged, his fentiments ennobled, and his whole
foul is elevated to fo great a degree, that, if the
abufes of this new ftate do not degrade him below the former, he ought inceffantly to blefs that
happy moment in which he was refcued from it,
and converted from a ftupid and ignorant animal
into an intelligent and wife Being.

To ftate the balance of what is loft and gained by this change, we fhall reduce it to compa-
rative terms. By entering into the focial compact, man gives up his natural liberty, or unlimited right to every thing which he is defirous of,
and can attain. In return for this, he gains focial liberty, and an exclufive property in all
thofe things of which he is poffeffed. To avoid
any miftake, however, in the nature of thefe
compenfations, it is neceffary to make a juft diftinction between natural liberty, which is limited

2

by

by nothing but the inabilities of the individual, and focial liberty, which is limited by the general will of the community; and alfo, between that poffeffion, which is only effected by force, or follows the right of prior occupancy, and that property, which is founded only on a pofitive title.

To the preceding alfo may be added, as the acquifition of a focial ftate, moral liberty, which only renders a man truly mafter of himfelf: for to be under the direction of appetite alone is to be in a ftate of flavery, while to pay obedience only to thofe laws which we prefcribe to ourfelves, is liberty. But I have faid too much already on this fubject, the philofophical meaning of the word Liberty being, in this place, out of the queftion.

C H A P. IX.

Of real demefnes.

EAch member of the community, in becoming fuch, devotes himfelf to the public from that moment, in fuch a ftate as he then is, with all his power and abilities, of which abilities his poffeffions make a part. Not that in confequence of this act the poffeffion changes its nature, by changing hands, and becomes actual

C 3   property

property in thofe of the fovereignty ; but as the power of the community is incomparably greater than that of an individual, the public poffeffion is in fact more fixed and irrevocable, without being more lawful, at leaft with regard to foreigners. For every ftate is, with refpect to its members, mafter of all their poffeffions, by virtue of the focial compact, which, in a ftate, ferves as the bafis of all other rights ; but, with regard to other powers or ftates, it is mafter of them only, by the right of prior occupancy, which it derives from individuals.

The right of prior occupancy, although more real than that of the ftrongeft, becomes not an equitable right, till after the eftablifhment of property. Every man hath naturally a right to every thing which is neceffary for his fubfiftence ; but the pofitive act by which he is made the proprietor of a certain poffeffion excludes him from the property of any other. His portion being affigned him, he ought to confine himfelf to that, and hath no longer any right to a community of poffeffion. Hence it is that the right of prior occupancy, though but of little force in a ftate of nature, is fo refpectable in that of fociety. The point to which we are chiefly directed in the confideration of this right, is rather

ther

ther what belongs to another, than what does not belong to us.

To define the right of prior occupancy in general terms, it is founded on the following conditions. It is requifite, in the firft place, that the lands in queftion fhould be unoccupied; fecondly, that no greater quantity of it fhould be occupied than is neceffary for the fubfiftence of the occupiers; and, in the third place, that pof-feffion fhould be taken of it, not by a vain ceremony, but by actual cultivation, the only mark of property, which, in defect of juridical titles, fhould be at all refpected.

To allow the firft occupier a right to as much territory as he may cultivate, and is neceffary to his fubfiftence, is certainly carrying the matter as far as is reafonable. Otherwife we know not how to fet bounds to this right. Is it fufficient for a man to fet foot on an uninhabited territory, to pretend immediately an exclufive right to it? Is it fufficient for him to have power enough at one time to drive others from the fpot, to deprive them for ever afterwards of the right of returning to it? How can a man, or even a whole people, poffefs themfelves of an immenfe territory, and exclude from it the reft of mankind, without

C 4   being

being guilty of an illegal ufurpation; fince, by fo doing, they deprive the reft of mankind of an habitation, and thofe means of fubfiftence, which nature hath given in common to them all? When Nunez Balbao ftood on the fea-fhore, and, in the name of the crown of Caftile, took poffef-fion of the Pacific Ocean, and of all South-America, was this fufficient to difpoffefs all the inhabitants of that vaft country, and exclude all the other fovereigns in the world? On fuch a fuppofition, the like idle ceremonies might have been ridiculoufly multiplied, and his Catholic Majefty would have had no more to do, than to have taken poffeffion in his clofet of all the coun-tries in the world, and to have afterwards only deducted from his empire fuch as were before poffeffed by other princes.

It is eafy to conceive, how the united and contiguous eftates of individuals become the ter-ritory of the public, and in what manner the right of fovereignty, extending itfelf from the fubjects to the lands they occupy, becomes at once both real and perfonal; a circumftance which lays the poffeffors under a ftate of the greateft dependence, and makes even their own abilities a fecurity for their fidelity. This is an
advantage

advantage which does not appear to have been duly attended to, by fovereigns among the ancients, who, by ftiling themfelves only kings of the Perfians, the Scythians, the Macedonians, feemed to look on themfelves only as chief of men, rather than as mafters of a country. Modern princes more artfully ftile themfelves the kings of England, France, Spain, &c. and thus, by claiming the territory itfelf, are fecure of the inhabitants.

What is very fingular in this alienation is, that the community, in accepting the poffeffions of individuals, is fo far from defpoiling them thereof, that, on the contrary, it only confirms them in fuch poffeffions, by converting an ufurpation into an actual right, and a bare poffeffion into a real property. The poffeffors alfo being confidered as the depofitaries of the public wealth, while their rights are refpected by all the members of the ftate, and maintained by all its force against any foreign power, they acquire, if I may fo fay, by a ceffion advantageous to the public, and ftill more fo to themfelves, every thing they ceded by it: a paradox which is eafily explained by the diftinction to be made between the rights which the fovereign and the

proprietor

proprietor have in the fame fund, as will be feen hereafter.

It may alfo happen, that men may form themfelves into a fociety, before they have any poffeffions; and that, acquiring a territory fufficient for all, they may poffefs it in common, or divide it among them, either equally, or in fuch different proportions as may be determined by the fovereign. Now, in whatfoever manner fuch acquifition may be made, the right which each individual has to his own eftate, muft be always fubordinate to the right which the community hath over the poffeffions of all; for, without this, there would be nothing binding in the focial tie, nor any real force in the exercife of the fupreme power.

I fhall end this book, with a remark, that ought to ferve as the bafis of the whole focial fyftem: and this is, that, inftead of annihilating the natural equality among mankind, the fundamental compact fubftitutes, on the contrary, a moral and legal equality, to make up for that natural and phyfical difference which prevails among individuals, who, though unequal in perfonal

fonal ftrength and mental abilities, become thus
all equal by convention and right *.

* This equality, indeed, is under fome governments merely apparent and delufive, ferving only to
keep the poor ftill in mifery, and favour the oppreffion of the rich. And, in fact, the laws are always
ufeful to perfons of fortune, and hurtful to thofe who
are deftitute: whence it follows, that a ftate of fociety is advantageous to mankind in general, only
when they all poffefs fomething, and none of them
have any thing too much.

The END of the FIRST BOOK.

C 6   BOOK

B O O K II.

CHAP. I.

That the sovereignty is unalienable.

THE firſt and moſt important conſequence to be drawn from the principles already eſtabliſhed, is, that the general *will* only can di-rect the forces of the ſtate agreeable to the end of its original inſtitution, which is the common good ; for, though the oppoſition of private in-tereſts might make the eſtabliſhment of ſocieties neceſſary, it muſt have been through the coali-tion of thoſe intereſts, that ſuch eſtabliſhment became poſſible. The bonds of ſociety muſt have been formed out of ſomething common to thoſe ſeveral intereſts, for, if there had been no point to which they could have been recon-ciled, no ſociety could poſſibly have ſubſiſted. Now it is only on theſe points that the govern-ment of ſociety ſhould be founded.

I ſay, therefore, that the ſovereignty, being only the exertion of the general will, cannot be alienated, and that the ſovereign, which is only a collective being, cannot be repreſented but by
itſelf :

itfelf: the power of a people may be tranfmitted or delegated, but not their will.

It may not be abfolutely impoffible, that the will of 'an individual fhould agree, in fome particular point, with the general will of a whole people ; it is, however, impoffible, that fuch agreement fhould be conftant and durable, for the will of particulars always tends to make diftinctions of preference, and the general will to a perfect equality. It is further ftill more impoffible, fuppofing fuch agreement might always fubfift, to have any fecurity that it would do fo, as it could never be the effect of art, but of chance. The fovereign may fay, My will is now agreeable to the will of fuch an individual, or at leaft to what he pretends to be his will ; but it cannot pretend to fay, I agree to whatever may be the will of fuch individual to-morrow ; as it is abfurd for the will to lay itfelf under any reftraint regarding the future, and as it is impoffible for the will to confent to any thing contrary to the intereft of the being whofe will it is. Should a people therefore enter into the engagement of fimply promifing obedience, they would lofe their quality, as a people, and be virtually diffolved by that very act. The moment there exifts a mafter, there can be no longer a fovereign, the body politic being thereby deftroyed.

I would

I would not be underftood to mean, that the
orders of a chief may not pafs for the dictates
of the general will, when the fovereign, though
at liberty to contradict, does not oppofe it. In
fuch a cafe, it is to be prefumed, from the uni-
verfal filence of the people, that they give their
confent. This will be farther explained in the
end.

CHAP. II.

That the fovereignty is indivifible.

FOR the fame reafon that the fovereignty is
unalienable, it is alfo indivifible ; for the
will is general *, or it is not ; it is that of the
body of the people, or only that of a part. In
the firft cafe, this will, when declared, is an act
of fovereignty, and becomes a law: in the fecond, it is only a particular will, or an act of the
magiftracy, and is at moft a decree.

But our politicians, incapable of dividing the
fovereignty in its firft principles, divide it in its

* In order that this will fhould be general, it is
not always neceffary it fhould be unanimous : it is neceffary, however, that every individual fhould be
permitted to vote ; every formal exclufion infringing
the generality.

object ;

object; they diftinguifh it into power and will ;. into a legiflative and executive power; into the prerogatives of taxation, of executing juftice, and of making war; into departments of do-meftic and foreign adminiftration. Sometimes they blend all thefe confufedly together, and, at others, confider them as diftinct and feparate, making out the fovereign to be a fantaftic com-pound, juft as if they fhould compofe a man out of feveral bodies, of which one fhould have on-ly eyes, another arms, a third feet, and nothing more. It is faid of the jugglers in Japan, that they will take a child, and cut it into pieces in the prefence of the fpectators, then, throwing up its difmembered limbs one after another into the air, they are united, and the child defcends alive, and well as before. The legerdemain of our modern politicians greatly refembles this trick of the Japonefe; for they, after having difmem-bered the body politic with equal dexterity,. bring all its parts together by *hocus pocus* again, and reprefent it the fame as before.

This error arifes from their not having form-ed precife ideas of the fovereign authority, and from their miftaking the fimple emanations of this authority, for parts of its effence. Thus, for inftance, the acts of declaring war and ma-king peace are ufually regarded as acts of fove--
reignty,.

reignty, which they are not; for neither of these acts are laws, but consist only of the application of the law. Each is a particular act, determinate only of the meaning of the law in such case, as will be seen more clearly, when the idea attached to the word *law* shall be precisely settled.

By tracing, in like manner, their other divisions, we shall find, that we are constantly mistaken, whenever we think the sovereignty divided; and that the prerogatives, which are supposed to be parts of the sovereignty, are all subordinate to it, and always suppose the predetermination of a superior will, which those prerogatives only serve to put in execution.

It is impossible to say, in how much obscurity this want of precision hath involved the reasonings of authors, on the subject of political law, when they came to examine into the respective rights of kings and people, on the principles they had established. By turning to the third and fourth chapters of the first book of Grotius, the reader may see, how that learned author and his translator, Barbeyrac, bewildered and entangled themselves in their own sophisms, through fear of saying too much or too little for their purpose, and of making those interests clash, which

which it was their bufinefs to reconcile. Grotius,
being diffatisfied with his own countrymen, a
refugee in France, and willing to pay his court
to Lewis XIII. to whom his book is dedicated,
fpared no art nor pains to ftrip the people of
their privileges, and to inveft kings with prerogative. Barbeyrac alfo wrote with a fimilar
view, dedicating his tranflation to George I. of
England. But, unluckily, the expulfion of
James II. which he calls an abdication, obliged
him to be much on the referve, to turn and
wind about, as he faw occafion, in order not to
make William III. an ufurper. Had thefe two
writers adopted true principles, all thefe difficulties would have vanifhed, and they would
have written confiftently; in fuch a cafe, however, they could only, in fober fadnefs, have told
the truth, and would have paid their court only
to the people. Now, to tell the truth, is not
the way to make a fortune; nor are ambaffadors
appointed, or places and penfions given away by
the populace.

CHAP.

CHAP. III.

Whether the general Will can be in the wrong.

IT follows, from what has been faid, that the general Will is always in the right, and conftantly tends to the public good; it does not follow, however, that the deliberations of the people will always be attended with the fame rectitude. We are ever defirous of our own good, but we do not always diftinguifh in what it confifts. A whole people never can be corrupted, but they may be often miftaken, and it is in fuch a cafe only that they appear to feek their own difadvantage.

There is often a confiderable difference between the will of all the members and the general will of the whole body; the latter regards only the common intereft, the other refpects the private intereft of individuals, and is the aggregated fum of their particular wills; but, if we take from this fum thofe contradictory wills that mutually deftroy each other *, the fum of the remaining differences is the general will.

If

* *Each intereft*, fays the Marquis d'A. *has different principles. A coalition between two particular interefts may be formed, out of oppofition to that of a third.* He might

If a people, sufficiently informed of the nature of the subject under their confideration,
fhould deliberate, without having any communication with each other, the general will would
always refult from the greater number of their
little differences, and their deliberation would
be fuch as it ought to be. But when they enter
into cabals, and form partial affociations, at the
expence of the general one, the will of each of
thefe affociations becomes general, with regard
to the particular members of each, and, in itfelf, particular, with regard to the ftate. In
fuch a cafe, therefore, it may be faid, there is
no longer as many voters as individuals, but only as many voices as there are affociations. The
differences then become lefs numerous, and give
a lefs general refult. Again, fhould one of thefe
partial affociations be fo great, as to influence all
the reft, the refult would no longer be the fum
of many little differences, but that of one
great one; in which cafe, a general will would
no longer fubfift.

might have added, that a coalition of all is formed
out of oppofition to the intereft of each. Were there
no different and clafhing interefts, that of the whole
would be hardly diftinguifhable, as it would meet
with no obftacle. All things would go regularly on
of their own accord, and civil policy would ceafe to
be an art.

It

It is requifite, therefore, in order that each re-
folution may be dictated by the general will,
that no fuch partial focieties fhould be formed in
a ftate, and that each citizen fhould think for
himfelf *. Such was the fublime inftitution of
the. great Lycurgus. But, if fuch partial focieties muft and will exift, it is then expedient
to multiply their number, and prevent their inequality, as was done by Solon, Numa, and
Servius. Thefe are the only falutary precautions
that can be taken, in order that the general will
may be properly informed, and the people not
be miftaken as to their true intereft.

CHAP. IV.

Of the limits of the fovereign power.

IF the ftate, or the city, be a mere moral
perfon, whofe life depends on the union of
its members, and, if the moft important of its
concerns be that of its own prefervation, it

* Vera cofa é, fays Machiavel, che alcuni divifi-
oni nuocono alle republiche, e alcune giovano : quel!e
nuocono che fono dalle fet:e e da partigiani accom-
pagnate : quelle giovano che fenza fette, fenza partigiani fi mantengono. Non potendo adunque prove-
dere un fondatore d'una republica che non fiano nimi-
cizie in quella, hà da provéder almeno che non vifia-
no fette. Hift. Fiorent. l. vii.

fhould

should certainly be possessed of an universal compulsive force, to move and dispose each part in such a manner as is most conducive to the good of all. As nature hath given every man an absolute power over his limbs, to move and direct them at pleasure, so the social compact gives to the body politic an absolute power over all its members, and it is this power which, directed by the general will, bears the name, as I have already observed, of the sovereignty.

But, besides this public person, we are to consider farther the private persons of which it is composed, and whose life and liberty are naturally independent of it. We come now, therefore, to make a proper distinction between the respective privileges of the citizens and the sovereign *, as well as between the obligations the former lie under as subjects, and the natural rights they claim as men.

It is agreed, that what an individual alienates of his power, his possession, or his liberty, by the social compact, is only such parts of them whose use is of importance to the community;

---

* Be not in haste, attentive reader, to accuse me here of contradiction. I cannot avoid the seeming contradiction in terms, from the native poverty of the language. But have a little patience.

but

but it muſt be confeſſed alſo, that the ſovereign is the only proper judge of this importance.

A citizen is bound to perform all the ſervices he can poſſibly be of to a ſtate, whenever the ſovereign demands them; but the ſovereign, on his part, cannot require any thing of the ſubject that is uſeleſs to the community; he cannot even be deſirous of ſo doing; for, under the laws of reaſon, nothing can be produced without a cauſe, any more than under the law of nature.

The engagements, in which we are bound to the body of ſociety, are obligatory, only becauſe they are mutual; and their nature is ſuch that we cannot, in diſcharging them, labour for the good of others, without, at the ſame time, labouring for that of ourſelves. Wherefore, indeed, is it, that the general will is always in the right, and that all conſtantly deſire the good of each, unleſs it be, becauſe there is no one that does not appropriate the term *each* to himſelf, and who does not think of his own intereſt, in voting for that of all? This ſerves to prove alſo, that an equality of privilege, and the notion of Juſtice it produces, are derived from that preference which each naturally gives himſelf, and of courſe from the very nature of man; that the

I

general

general will, in order to be truly fuch, ought to be fo in its effect, as well as in its effence; that it ought to flow from all, in order to be applicable to all; and that it muft lofe its natural rectitude, when it tends to any individual and determinate object; becaufe judging, in fuch a cafe, of what is foreign to ourfelves, we have no real principle of equity for our guide.

In fact, no fooner do we come to treat of a particular fact or privilege, on a point which has not been fettled by a general and prior convention, than the affair becomes litigious. It is a procefs, in which the particulars interefted are one party, and the public the other; but in which I fee no law to decide, nor judge to determine. It would be abfurd, therefore, in fuch a cafe, to think of referring it to any exprefs decifion of the general will, which could be no other than the decifion of one of the very parties; and therefore muft be, with regard to the other, foreign and partial, leaning to injuftice, and fubject to error. In the fame manner, alfo, that a partial and particular will cannot reprefent the general will, fo the latter, in its turn, changes its nature, when employed on a particular object, and cannot, in its general capacity, pronounce concerning any particular man or fact. Thus, when the people of Athens, for inftance,

took

took upon them to appoint or cafhier their chiefs, to decree honours to one, and inflict pains and penalties on another, and thus, by numerous decrees, exercifed indifcriminately all the acts of government, they had then, properly fpeaking, no general will at all: the Athenian people, in this cafe, did not act in the capacity of fovereign, but in that of magiftrate. This may appear contradictory to the common notions of things, but I muft be allowed time to explain mine.

We may learn hence, that the general will confifts lefs in the number of votes, than in the common intereft that unites them ; for, in this inftitution, every one fubjects himfelf necefTarily to thofe conditions which he impofes on others : hence the admirable conformity between intereft and juftice, which ftamps on public declarations that characteriftic of equity, which we fee vanifh in the difcuffion of particular fubjects, for want of that common intereft which unites and makes the criterion of the judge the fame with that of the party.

In what manner foever we recur to the firft principle, we always arrive at the fame conclu-, fion, viz. that the focial compact, eftablifhes fuch an equality among the citizens, that all lay
themfelves

themselves under the same obligations, and ought all to enjoy the same privileges. Thus, from the very nature of this compact, every act of sovereignty, that is to say, every authentic act of the general will, is equally obligatory on, or favourable to, all the citizens, without distinction; in so much that the sovereign knows only the whole body of the nation, but distinguishes none of the individuals who compose it. What then is properly an act of sovereignty? It is not an agreement made between a superior and an inferior, but a convention between a whole body with each of its members, which convention is a lawful one, because founded on the social contract; it is equitable, because it is common to all; it is useful, because it can have no other object than the general good; and it is solid and durable, because secured by the public strength and the supreme power.

When the submission of subjects is owing only to such conventions, they pay in fact obedience to none but their own will, and to ask how far the respective privileges of the sovereign and citizens extend, is to ask merely how far the latter may enter into engagements with themselves, *viz.* each individual with all collectively, and all collectively with each individual.

D

Hence

Hence we fee, that the fovereign power, abfolute, inviolable, and facred as it is, neither does nor can furpafs the bounds of fuch general conventions, and that every man hath a right to difpofe, as he pleafes, of that liberty and property which the terms of fuch conventions have left to his own difpofal; fo that the fovereign hath not any right to lay a greater burthen on one fubject than on another, becaufe, in fuch a cafe, it becomes a particular affair, in which the fovereign hath no power to act.

Thefe diftinctions being once admitted, it is fo far from being true, that there is any real renunciation on the part of individuals, when they enter into the focial compact, that their fituation becomes, by means of that very compact, much better than before; as, inftead of making any alienation, they only make an advantageous exchange of an uncertain and precarious mode of fubfiftence, for a more fettled and determinate one; they exchange their natural independence, for focial liberty, the power of injuring others for that of fecuring themfelves from injury; and their own natural ftrength, which might be overcome by that of others, for a civil power which the focial union renders invincible. Their very lives, which they have by thefe means de-

devoted to the ftate, are continually protected; and even when they are obliged to expofe themfelves to death, in its defence, what do they more than render back to fociety what they have before received of it? What do they more, in rifquing their lives for their country, than they would have been obliged to do more frequently, and with much greater danger in a ftate of nature; when, fubject to inevitable outrages, they would have been obliged to defend their means of fubfiftance at the hazard of their lives?

That every one lies under the obligation of fighting in defence of his country, is true; but then he is relieved by the laws from the neceffity of fighting to defend himfelf. And are not men gainers, on the whole, by running part of thofe rifks, for their common fecurity, which they muft feverally run for themfelves, were they deprived of that fecurity?

CHAP. V.

On capital punifhments.

IT hath been afked, how individuals, having no right to difpofe of their own lives, can tranfmit that right to the fovereign? The difficulty of refolving this queftion, arifes only from

its

its being badly expreffed. Every man hath an un-
doubted right to hazard his life for its prefervation.
Was a man ever charged with fuicide, for throwing himfelf from the top of an houfe in flames, in
order to avoid being burnt? Was it ever im-
puted as a crime to a man, who might be caft
away at fea, that he knew the danger of the
voyage when he embarked ?

The end of the focial compact, is the prefervation of the contracting parties.   Such,
therefore, as would reap the benefit of the end,
muft affent to the means, which are infeparable
from fome dangers and loffes. He that would preferve his life at the expence of others, ought
to rifk it for their fafety when it is neceffary.
Now, the citizen is no longer a judge of the danger to which the law requires him to be expofed :
but when the prince declares that the good of
the ftate requires his life, he ought to refign it;
fince it is only on thofe conditions he hath hitherto lived in fecurity, and his life is not
folely the gift of nature, but a conditional gift
of the ftate.

The punifhment of death inflicted on malefactors may be confidered alfo in the fame point
of view : it is to prevent our falling by the
hands

hands of an affaffin, that we confent to die, on becoming fuch ourfelves. We are fo far from giving away our lives, by this treaty, that we enter into it only for our prefervation : as it is not to be prefumed that any one of the contracting parties formed therein a premeditated defign to get himfelf hanged.

Add to this, that every malefactor, by breaking the laws of his country, becomes a rebel and traitor; ceafing, from that time, to be a member of the community, and even declaring war againft it. In this cafe, the prefervation of the ftate is incompatible with his; one of the two muft perifh: and thus when a criminal is executed, he doth not fuffer in the quality of a citizen, but in that of an enemy. His trial and fentence are the evidence and declaration of his having broken the focial compact, and that, of confequence, he is no longer a member of the ftate. Now, as he had profeffed himfelf fuch, at leaft by his refidence, it is right that he fhould be feparated from the ftate, either by banifhment as a violator of the focial compact, or by death as a public enemy; for fuch an enemy is not a moral perfonage, he is a mere man, and it is in this cafe only that the right of war takes place of killing an enemy.

But,

But, it may be faid, the condemnation of a criminal is a particular act. It is fo, and for that reafon it does not belong to the fovereign: it is an act, for doing which the fupreme power may confer the authority, though it cannot ex-ercife fuch authority itfelf. My ideas on this fubject are confiftent, though I cannot explain them all at once.

It is to be obferved, however, that the fre-quency of executions is always a fign of the weaknefs or indolence of government. There is no malefactor who might not be made good for fomething: Nor ought any perfon to be put to death, even by way of example, unlefs fuch as could not be preferved without endangering the community.

With regard to the prerogative of granting pardons to criminals, condemned by the laws of their country, and fentenced by the judges, it belongs only to that power which is fuperior both to the judges and the laws, viz. the fove-reign authority. Not that it is very clear that even the fupreme power is vefted with fuch a right, or that the circumftances in which it might be exerted are frequent or determinate. In a well-governed ftate there are but few executions;

tions; not becaufe there are many pardoned, but
becaufe there are few criminals: Whereas when
a ftate is on the decline, the multiplicity of
crimes occafions their impunity. Under the
Roman republic, neither the Senate nor the Confuls ever attempted to grant pardons; even the
people never did this, although they fometimes
recalled their own fentence. The frequency
of pardons indicates that in a fhort time crimes
will not ftand in need of them, and every one may
fee the confequence of fuch conduct. But my
reluctant heart reftrains my pen; let us leave the
difcuffion of thefe queftions to the juft man
who hath never been criminal, and who never
ftood in need of pardon.

CHAP. VI.

On the law.

HAVING given exiftence and life to the
body politic, by a focial compact, we
come now to give it action and will, by a legiflature. For the primitive act, by which fuch
body is formed, determines nothing as yet with
refpect to the means of its prefervation.

Whatever is right and conformable to order,
is fuch from the nature of things, independent

D 4

of

of all human conventions. All juſtice comes from God, who is the fountain of it; but could we receive it immediately from ſo ſublime a ſource, we ſhould ſtand in no need of government or laws. There is indeed an univerſal juſtice ſpring-ing from reaſon alone; but, in order to admit this to take place among mankind, it ſhould be reciprocal. To conſider things as they appear, we find the maxims of juſtice among mankind, to be vain and fruitleſs, for want of a natural ſupport; they tend only to the advantage of the wicked, and the diſadvantage of the juſt, while the latter obſerves them in his behavour to others, but no body regards them in their conduct to him. Laws and conventions, therefore, are neceſſary in order to unite duties with privileges, and confine juſtice to its proper objects. In a ſtate of nature, where every thing is common, I owe nothing to thoſe I have promiſed nothing; I acknowlege nothing to be the property of an-other, but what is uſeleſs to myſelf. In a ſtate of ſociety the caſe is different, where the rights of each are fixed by law.

We come at length, therefore, to conſider what is law. So long as we content ourſelves with the metaphyſical idea annexed to this term, we muſt talk unintelligibly; and though we
ſhould

fhould come to a definition of natural law, we fhould not know thence any thing more of political law. I have already faid there can be no general will relative to a particular object. In fact every particular object muft be within or without the ftate. If without, a will that is foreign, cannot with regard to it be general; and if the object be within the ftate, it muft make a part of it: in which cafe there arifes between the whole and the part, a relation that conftitutes two feparate beings, one of which is the part, and the whole wanting fuch part, is the other. But the whole wanting fuch part, is not the whole, and fo long as that relation fubfifts, there is no whole, but only two unequal parts: whence it follows that the will of the one is no longer general with regard to that of the other.

But when a whole people decree concerning a whole people, they confider only their whole body; and, if it then forms any relation, it muft be between the entire object confidered in one point of view, and the entire object confidered in another point of view, without any divifion of the whole. In this cafe, the matter of the decree is general as the will that decrees. Such is the act which I call a law.

D 5.   When

When I fay that the object of the laws is always general, I mean that the law confiders the
fubjects in a collective body, and their actions
abftractedly, but never concerns itfelf with individual perfons, nor particular actions. Thus
the law may decree certain privileges, but it
cannot beftow them on particular perfons : the
law may conftitute feveral claffes of citizens,
and affign even the qualities which may entitle
them to rank in thefe claffes ; but it cannot nominate fuch or fuch perfons to be admitted
therein: It may eftablifh a legal government,
and appoint an hereditary fucceffion, but it cannot make choice of a king, nor appoint the royal
family ; in a word, every function that relates to
an individual object, doth not belong to the legiflative power.

Taking things in this light, it is immediately
feen how abfurd it is to afk in whofe power it is
to make laws ? as they are acts of the general
will ; or whether the prince be above the laws ?
as he is but a member of the ftate. Hence alfo,
it is plain, the law cannot be unjuft, as nothing
can be unjuft to itfelf; as alfo what it is to be
free, and at the fame time fubject to the laws,
as the laws are only the records of our own
will.

It

It is hence farther evident, the law re-uniting the univerfality of the will to that of its object that whatever an individual, of what rank foever, may decree of his own head, cannot be a law: indeed, whatever the fupreme power itfelf may ordain concerning a particular object is not a law, but a fimple decree; it is not an act of the fovereignty, but of the magiftracy.

I call every ftate, therefore, which is governed by laws, a Republic, whatever be the form of its adminiftration; for in fuch a cafe only, it is the public intereft that governs, and whatever is public is fomething. Thus every lawful government is republican *. I fhall explain hereafter what I mean by a government.

The laws are, ftrictly fpeaking, only the conditions of civil fociety. The people who fub-

* I do not here mean, by the term republican, either an ariftocracy or democracy; but in general every government influenced by the general will of the people, which is the law. To make a government legal, it is not neceffary that it fhould be confounded with the fovereign, but that it fhould be the minifter; fo that in this fenfe even a monarchy is a republic. This will be more fully explained in the fubfequent book.

mit

mit to them should therefore be the authors of
them; as it certainly belongs to the associating
parties, to settle the conditions on which they
agree to form a society. But how are they to
be settled? is it to be done by common consent
or by a sudden inspiration? hath the body politic an organ by which to make known its will?
who shall furnish it with the necessary prescience
to form its determinations, and to publish them
before-hand, or how shall it divulge them in the
time of need? how shall an ignorant multitude,
who often know not what they chuse, because
they seldom know what is for their good, execute an enterprize so great and so difficult as
that of a system of legislature? A people must
necessarily be desirous of their own good, but
they do not always see in what it consists. The
general will is always in the right, but the
judgment by which it is directed is not always
sufficiently informed. It is necessary it should
see objects such as they are, and sometimes such
as they ought to appear; it should be directed
to the salutary end it would pursue, should be
secured from the seduction of private interests,
should have an insight into the circumstances
of time and place; and should be enabled to
set the present and perceptible advantages of
things, against the distant and concealed evil
that

that may attend them. Individuals often fee the good which they reject; the public is de_firous of that which it is incapable to fee. Both ftand equally in need of a guide: the former fhould be compelled to conform their defires to reafon, and the latter fhould be inftructed in the difcovery of what it defires. It is thus from the proper information of the public, that there re_fults an union of the underftanding and the will in the body of fociety, and thence the exact concurrence of its parts, and in the end the greateft force of the whole. Hence arifes the neceffity of a legiflator.

C H A P. VII.

Of the genius and character of a legiflator.

TO inveftigate thofe conditions of fociety which may beft anfwer the purpofes of nations, would require the abilities of fome fu_perior intelligence, who fhould be witnefs to all the paffions of men, but be fubject itfelf to none; who fhould have no connection with human nature, but fhould have a perfect know_lege of it; a being, in fhort, whofe happi_nefs fhould be independent of us, and who

would

would neverthelefs employ itfelf about ours *.
It is the province of Gods indeed to make laws
for men.

The fame argument which Caligula made ufe
of, in point of fact, Plato himfelf employs, in
point of right, when he goes about to define the civil or royal perfonage, in treating of
a king. But if it be certain that a great prince
is a perfonage rarely to be met with, what is
that of a great legiflator ? The former hath nothing more to do than to follow the model defigned by the latter. The one is the mechanical
genius who invents the machine, the other only
the workman who puts it into execution. In
the commencement of focieties, fays Montefquieu, it is the principal perfons in republics
which form their inftitution ; and afterwards it
is the inftitution which forms the chiefs of republics.

He who fhould undertake to form a body politic, ought to perceive himfelf capable of work-
ing a total change in human nature; of tranf-
forming every individual, of himfelf a folitary

* Nations become famous only as their legiflature
declines. The inftitution of Lycurgus made the
Spartan, happy for ages before they were famous in
Greece.

and

and independent being, into a part of a greater whole, from which such individual is to receive in one sense his life and exiftence; he muft be capable of altering the conftitution of the man, in order to ftrengthen it; and to fubftitute a partial and moral exiftence in the room of that phyfical and independent exiftence which we receive from the hands of Nature. In a word, he muft be able to deprive man of his natural abilities, in order to inveft him with foreign powers which he cannot make ufe of without the affiftance of others. The more fuch natural force is annihilated and extinct, the greater and more durable are thofe which are acquired, and the more perfect and folid is the focial inftitution. So that if each citizen be nothing, and can effect nothing but by the exiftence and affiftance of all the reft, and that the force acquired by the whole body be equal, or fuperior, to the fum of the natural forces of all its individuals, the legiflature may be faid to have reached the higheft pitch of perfection it is capable to attain.

The legiflator is in every refpect a moft extraordinary perfon in a ftate. If he be undoubtedly fo, on account of his genius, he is not lefs fo from his function. Yet this is not that of the

ma-

magiftrate or the fovereign.   That function,
which conftitutes the republic, doth not enter
into its conftitution.   It is, on the contrary,
a particular and fuperior employment that hath
nothing in common with human government :
for if he who hath the command over the citizens,
fhould not be entrufted with the command over
the laws, he who hath the power over the laws,
ought as little to have the power over the citizens : for were it otherwife, his laws, being made
inftrumental to his paffions, would often ferve to
perpetuate his injuftice, and he could never prevent particular views from altering his fyftem.

When Lycurgus gave laws to his country, he
began by abdicating the throne.   It was the
cuftom of moft of the Grecian cities to entruft
their eftablifhment with ftrangers ; a cuftom
that hath been often imitated by the modern
republics of Italy : that of Geneva did the fame,
and found its account in it *.   In the moft

* Thofe who confider Calvin only as a theologift,
know but little of his comprehenfive genius.   The
digeft of our laws, in which he had a confiderable fhare, do him as much honour as his religious
fyftem ; and what revolution foever time may effect
in our public worfhip, the memory of this great man
will continue to be revered fo long as patriotifm and
a fenfe of liberty furvive among us.

flourifhflourishing age of Rome, that city suffered under flagitious acts of tyranny, and beheld itself on the brink of ruin, for having entrusted the sovereign power and the legislative authority in the same hands.

Even the decemviri themselves, however, never assumed the right of passing any law merely on their own authority. *Nothing that we propose*, said they to the people, *can pass into a law without your consent. Be yourselves, ye Romans, the authors of those laws on which your happiness depends.*

The legislator, therefore, who digests the laws, should have no right to make them pass for such; nor indeed can the people, though inclined to do it, deprive themselves of that incommunicable right : because, according to the fundamental compact, it is the general will only that is obligatory on individuals, and it is impossible to be assured that any particular will is conformable to the general, till it be submitted to on the free suffrage of the people. I have said this before, but perhaps have not unnecessarily repeated it.

Thus.

Thus in the bufinefs of a legiflature, we find two things apparently incompatible; a defign fuperior to human abilities, carried into execution by an authority which is nothing.

Another difficulty which merits attention is, that wife men, in talking their own language to the vulgar, fpeak unintelligibly. · And yet there are many kinds of ideas which it is impoffible to convey in the language of the people. Views too general, and objects too diftant, are equally beyond their comprehenfion; the individual, relifhing no other plan of government than that which is conducive to his private intereft, is with difficulty brought to fee thofe advantages which are to be deduced from the continual checks he may receive from falutary laws. In order to give a newly-formed people a tafte for the found maxims of policy, and induce them to follow the fundamental rules of fociety, it is neceffary that the effect fhould in a manner become the caufe; that the fpirit of union which fhould be the effect of focial inftitutions fhould prefide to form that inftitution itfelf, and that men fhould be fuch before the laws are made as the laws are defigned to make them. For this reafon therefore, the legiflator being capable of employing neither force nor argument, he he is of neceffity obliged to recur to an authority of an higher order, which may compel without violence, and perfuade without conviction. Hence it is that the founders of nations have been obliged, in all ages, to recur to the intervention of celeftial powers, and have honoured their gods with their own wifdom, in order that the people, by fubmitting themfelves to the laws of the ftate in the fame manner as to thofe of nature, and acknowleging the fame power in the formation of the city as in the formation of man, might bend more freely, and bear more tractably the yoke of obedience and public felicity.

Now the determinations of that fublime reafon, which foars above the comprehenfion of vulgar minds, are thofe which the legiflator puts into the mouths of his immortal perfonages, in order to influence thofe by a divine authority, which could not be led by maxims of human prudence. It does not belong to every man, however, to make the gods his oracles, nor even to be believed when he pretends to be their interpreter. The comprehenfive genius of the legiflator, is the miracle that proves the truth of his miffion. Any man may engrave tables of ftone, hire an oracle, pretend to a fecret communica-

munication with some deity, teach a bird to
whisper in his ear, or hit upon other devices
to impose on a people. But he who knows nothing more, though he may be lucky enough to
get together an assembly of fools and madmen,
will never lay the foundations of an Empire ;
the fabrick raised by his extravagance presently
falling and often burying him in its ruins. A
transitory union may be formed from slight and
futile connections ; nothing but the dictates of
wisdom, however, can render it durable. The
Jewish law, still subsisting, and that of the son of
Ismael, which for ten centuries hath governed
half the world, are standing proofs of the superior genius of those great men by whom they
were dictated : and though the vanity of phi-
losophy, and the blind prejudice of party see
nothing in their characters but fortunate im-
postors, the true politician admires, in their respective institutions, that sagacious and com-
prehensive power of mind which must ever lay
the lasting foundation of human establishments.

It must not, from all this, be concluded, however, that religion and government have, in our
times, as Warburton alleges, one common object ; but only that in the first establishment of
societies, the one was made instrumental to the
other.   C H A P.

CHAP. VIII.

Of the people.

AS the architect, before he begins to raise an edifice, examines into the ground where he is to lay the foundation, that he may be able to judge whether it will bear the weight of the superstructure; so the prudent legislator does not begin by making a digest of salutary laws, but examines first whether the people for whom such laws are designed, are capable of supporting them. It was for this reason Plato refused to give laws to the Arcadians and Cyrenians, knowing they were rich and luxurious, and could not admit of the introduction of equality among them. It was for this reason that Crete, though it boasted good laws, was inhabited by such bad men; Minos had only endeavoured to govern a people already depraved by vice. Various have been the nations that have made a distinguished figure in the world, and yet have not been capable of being governed by good laws; and even those who were capable of being so governed, continued so but a short time. Nations, as well as individuals, are docile only in their infancy : they

be-

become incorrigible as they grow old. When cuftoms are once eftablifhed and prejudices have taken root among them, it is a dangerous and fruitlefs enterprize to attempt to reform them. A people cannot even bear to have their wounds probed, though in order to be cured ; but refemble thofe weak and cowardly patients who fhudder at the fight of their phyfician. Not, but that fometimes, as there are diftempers which affect the brain of individuals and deprive them of the capacity of remembering what is paft, there happen in ftates fuch revolutions as produce the fame effect on a people, when the horror of the paft fupplies the place of oblivion, and the ftate, inflamed and exhaufted by civil wars, rifes again, if I may fo exprefs myfelf, out of its own afhes, and reaffumes the vigour of youth in forfaking the arms of death. This was the cafe with Sparta in the time of Lycurgus, and of Rome after the Tarquins ; and fuch hath been the cafe in modern times with Holland and Switzerland after the expulfion of their tyrants. But thefe events are rare ; and are fuch exceptions as have their caufe in the particular conftitution of the ftate excepted. They cannot even take place twice among the fame people : for though they may be made free when they are only barbarous and

un-

uncivilized; yet, when the refources of fociety are exhaufted, they cannot be renewed. In that cafe, faction may deftroy, but revolutions cannot re-eftablifh their freedom; they require for ever after a mafter, and not a deliverer. Every free people, therefore, fhould remember this maxim, that tho' nations may acquire liberty, yet if once this ineftimable acquifition is loft, it is abfolutely irrecoverable.

There is in nations, as well as individuals, a term of maturity, at which they fhould be permitted to arrive before they are fubjected to laws. This term, however, is not always eafy to be known; and yet if it be anticipated it may be of dangerous confequence. Again, one people may be formed to difcipline in their infancy; while another may not be ripened for fubjection till after many centuries. The Ruffians, for inftance, will never be truly polifhed becaufe they were difciplined too foon. Peter had only an imitative turn; he had nothing of that true genius, whofe creative power forms things out of nothing. Some of his meafures, indeed, were proper enough, but moft of them were ill-timed or ill-placed. He faw that his fubjects were mere barbarians, but he did not

fee

fee that they were not ripe for being made polite. He wanted to civilize them, when he fhould
only have checked their brutality. He wanted
to make them, at once, Germans and Englifh-
men, whereas he ought to have begun by
making them firft Ruffians; and thus he prevented his fubjects from ever becoming what
otherwife they might have been, by per-
fuading them they were fuch as they were
not. It is thus a French tutor forms his pupil
to make a figure in his child-hood, and to
make none for ever afterwards. The Empire
of Ruffia, while it is ambitious of reducing all
Europe to its fubjection, will be fubjected
itfelf. Its neighbours, the Tartars, will in time
become both its mafters and ours. This event
feems to me inevitable; all the monarchs in
Europe feeming to act, in concert, to accelerate
fuch a revolution.

CHAP. IX.

The fubject continued.

IN the fame manner as nature hath limited
the dimenfions of a well-formed human
body, beyond which fhe produces only giants
or dwarfs, fo in the body politic there are
limits,

limits, within or beyond which a ſtate ought not to be confined or extended; to the end that it may not be too big to be well governed, nor too little to maintain its own independency. There is in every body politic a *maximum* of force which it cannot exceed, and from which it often recedes by extending its dominion. The more the ſocial knot is extended, the more lax it grows; and in general, a little ſtate is always proportionably ſtronger than a great one.

A thouſand reaſons might be given in ſupport of this maxim. In the firſt place, the adminiſtration of government becomes always more difficult as the diſtance from the ſeat of it increaſes, even as a body has the greateſt weight at the end of the longeſt lever. It becomes alſo more burthenſome in proportion as it is divided into parts; for every town hath firſt its own particular government to pay; that of each diſtrict again is paid by the ſame people; next that of the province, then that of particular governments with their viceroys, all of whom are to be paid as they riſe in dignity, and always at the expence of the unhappy people; whom, laſt of all, the ſupreme adminiſtration itſelf cruſhes with the whole weight of its oppreſſion. It is impoſſible ſo many

need-

needlefs charges fhould not tend continually to impoverifh the people ; who, fo far from being better governed by thefe different ranks of fuperiors, are much worfe fo, than if they had but one order of governors in the ftate. And yet with this multiplicity of rulers, they are far from being furnifhed with proper re-fources for extraordinary occafions ; but, on the contrary, when they have occafion to recur to them, the ftate is always on the brink of ruin.

Nor is this all ; the government not only be-comes lefs vigorous and active in putting the laws in execution, removing private oppreffion, correcting abufes, or preventing the feditious enterprifes of rebellion in diftant provinces ; but the people have lefs affection for their chiefs, whom they never have an opportunity to fee ; for their country, which to them is like the whole world ; and for their fellow-fubjects, of which the greater part are utter ftrangers. The fame laws cannot be convenient for fo many various people of different manners, and cli-mates, and who cannot be fuppofed to live equally happy under the fame form of govern-ment. And yet different laws muft occafion much

much trouble and confusion among people, who, living under the same administration, and carrying on a perpetual intercourse, frequently change their habitations, inter marry with each other, and, being educated under different cuftoms, hardly ever know when their property is fecure. Great talents lie buried, virtue lives obfcured, and vice prevails with impunity, amidft that multitude of ftrangers, which flock together round the chief feat of adminiftration. The principals, overwhelmed with a multiplicity of bufinefs, can look into nothing themfelves; the government of the ftate being left to their deputies and clerks. In a word, the meafures to be taken, in order to maintain the general authority, on which fo many diftant officers are ever ready to encroach or impofe, engrofs the public attention; there is none of it left to be employed about the happinefs of the people, and indeed hardly any for their defence in cafe of need: thus it is, that a body too unwieldy for its conftitution grows debilitated and finks under its own weight.

On the other hand, a ftate ought to be fixed on fome bafis, to fecure its folidity, to be able to refift thofe fhocks which it will not fail to encounter, and to make thofe efforts which it

will

will find neceffary to maintain its independence.
Nations have all a kind of centrifugal force by
which they act continually againft each other,
and tend, like the vortices of Defcartes, to aggran-
dize themfelves at the expence of their neighbours. Thus the weak run in danger of being
prefently fwallowed up by the ftrong ; nor is
there any fecurity for them, but by keeping
themfelves in equilibrio with the reft, and making the compreffion on every fide equal.

Hence we fee it is prudent in fome cafes to
extend, and in others to reftrain, the limits of a
ftate ; nor is it one of the leaft arts in civil polity to diftinguifh between one and the other,
and to fix on that advantageous proportion
which tends moft to the prefervation of the
ftate. It may be obferved in general, that the
reafons for extending dominion, relating to objects external and relative, ought to be fubordinate to thofe for contracting it, whofe objects
are internal and abfolute. A found and vigorous
conftitution is the firft thing to be confidered,
and a much greater reliance is to be made on a
good government, than on the refources which
are to be drawn from an extenfive territory.

Not

Not but that there have been inflances of flates fo conftituted, that the neceffity of their making conquefts hath been effential to their very conftitution. It is poffible alfo they might felicitate themfelves on that happy neceffity, which pointed out, neverthelefs, with the fummit of their grandeur, the inevitable moment of their fall.

CHAP. X.

The fubject continued.

THE magnitude of a body politic may be taken two ways; viz. by the extent of territory, and the number of the people; a certain proportional relation between them conflituting the real greatnefs of a flate. It is the people which form the flate, and the territory which affords fubfiftence to the people; this relation, therefore, exifts when the territory is fufficient for the fobfiftence of the inhabitants, and the inhabitants are as numerous as the territory can maintain. In this proportion confifts the *maximum* of the force of any given number of people; for if the territory be too extenfive, the defence of it is burthenfome, the cultivation infufficient, and the produce fuper-

E 3   flúous;

fluous; hence the proximate caufes of defenfive
war. If, on the other hand, the territory be too
fmall, the ftate is under the neceffity of being
obliged for part of its fubfiftence to its neighbours; hence the proximate caufes of offenfive
war. Every people who, by their fituation,
have no other alternative than commerce or
war, muft be neceffarily feeble: they muft depend on their neighbours, on adventitious circumftances, and can only have a fhort and uncertain exiftence. They muft conquer others,
and thereby change their fituation, or be conquered themfelves, and thence be reduced to nothing. It is impoffible fuch a ftate can preferve
its independency but by its infignificancy or its
greatnefs.

It is not eafy to calculate the determinate relation between the extent of territory and number of inhabitants, fufficient for each other;
not only on account of the difference in the qualities of the foil, in its degrees of fertility, in
the nature of its productions, and in the influence of climate, but alfo on account of the remarkable difference in the temperament and conftitution of the inhabitants; fome confuming but
little in a fertile country, and others a great deal
on a barren foil. Regard muft alfo be had to

the

the degree of fecundity among the females, to the circumstances favourable or deftructive to population, and to the number of people which the legiflator may hope to draw from other countries by the advantages attending his fcheme of government; fo that he ought not to found his judgment on what actually exifts; but on what he forefees may exift hereafter; not on the prefent ftate of population, but on that which will naturally fucceed. In fine, there are a thoufand occafions, on which local accidents acquire, or permit, a ftate to poffefs a larger fhare of territory than may appear actually neceffary for prefent ufe. Thus a people may fpread themfelves over a large fpot in a mountainous country, whofe natural produce, of wood or pafture, requires lefs labour of cultivation; where experience teaches us that women are more fruitful than in the flat countries; and in which a large inclined fuperficies gives but a fmall horizontal bafe, by which only the land muft be eftimated in the affair of vegetation. A people, on the contrary, may inhabit a lefs fpace on the fea-fhore, or even among rocks and almoft barren fands; becaufe the fifhery fupplies them with fuftenance, inftead of the produce of the earth; they can eafily difburthen their community by fending

E 4   out

out colonies of its fupernumerary inhabitants;
and laftly, becaufe it is neceffary for them in fuch
a cafe to live near to each other, in order to repel the invafions of pyrates.

We may add to thefe conditional precautions,
refpecting the formation of a people, one that
can be fupplied by no other, but without which
all the reft are ufelefs : this is, that they fhould
enjoy peace and plenty. For the time in which
a ftate is forming, refembles that in which
foldiers are forming a battalion ; it is the moment in which they are leaft capable of refiftance, and the moft eafily defeated. They would
even make a greater refiftance when put into
abfolute diforder afterwards, than during the in-
terval of their firft fermentation, when each is
taken up more about his own particular rank than
the common danger. Should a war, a famine,
or a rebellion, break out at fuch a crifis, the ftate
would be infallibly fubverted.

Not but there have been many governments
eftablifhed in times of diforder and confufion : in fuch cafes, however, thofe very governments fubverted the ftate. Ufurpers
have always given rife to, or took the advantage of, thofe times of general confufion, in order

der to procure such destructive laws, which
the people never could have been prevailed on
to pass at a more dispassionate season. The
choice of the proper time for the institution of
laws, is one of the most certain tokens by which
we may distinguish the design of a legislator
from that of a tyrant.

If it be asked then, what people are in a
situation to receive a system of laws? I answer,
those who, though connected by some primitive
union either of interest or compact, are not
yet truly subjected to regular laws; those whose
customs and prejudices are not deeply rooted;
those who are under no fear of being swallowed
up by a sudden invasion, and who, without
entering into the quarrels of their neighbours,
are able to encounter separately with each, or to
engage the assistance of one to repel the other;
a people whose individuals may be known to
each other, and among whom it is not necessary to charge a man with a greater burthen
than it is possible for him to bear; a people
who can subsist without others, and without
whom all others might subsist *; a people neither

* If two neighbouring people were so situated that
one could not subsist without the other, the circum-

stances

ther rich nor poor, but poſſeſſed of a compe-
tence within themſelves ; a people, in ſhort,
who poſſeſs at once the conſiſtency of an ancient nation, and the docility of a newly-created
one. The great difficulty in legiſlation, con-
ſiſts leſs in knowing what ought to be eſtabliſhed
than what ought to be eradicated ; and what
renders it ſo ſeldom ſucceſsful, is the impoſſibi-
lity of finding the ſimplicity of nature in the
wants of ſociety. It is true that all theſe circumſtances are very rarely united ; and it is for
this reaſon that ſo few ſtates have much to
boaſt of, in their conſtitution. There is ſtill
one country in Europe capable of receiving
laws : this is the iſland of Corſica. The valour and conſtancy, with which thoſe brave
people recovered, and have defended their liber-

ſtances of the firſt would be very hard, and of the latter
very dangerous. Every wiſe nation, in ſuch a caſe,
would extricate itſelf as ſoon as poſſible from ſuch
a ſtate of dependence. ⋅ The republic of Thlaſcala,
ſituated in the heart of the Mexican empire, choſe
rather to be without ſalt than purchaſe it, or even
receive it gratis of the Mexicans. The prudent
Thlaſcalans ſaw through the ſnare of ſuch liberality.
Thus they preſerved their liberty ; this petty ſtate,
included within that great empire, being, in the end,
the cauſe of its ruin.

ty,

ty, might defervedly excite fome wife man to teach them how to preferve it. I cannot help furmifing, that this little ifland will, one day or other, be the aftonifhment of Europe.

CHAP. XI.

Of the various fyftems of legiflature.

IF we were to enquire, in what confifts precifely the greateft good, or what ought to be the end of every fyftem of legiflature; we fhould find it reducible to two principal objects, *liberty* and *equality*; liberty, becaufe all partial dependence deprives the whole body of the ftate of fo much ftrength; equality, becaufe liberty cannot fubfift without it.

I have already explained the nature of focial liberty; and with regard to equality, we are not to underftand by that term, that individuals fhould all abfolutely poffefs the fame degree of wealth and power; but only that, with refpect to the latter, it fhould never be exercifed contrary to good order and the laws; and with refpect to the former, that no one citizen fhould be rich enough to buy another, and that none fhould be fo poor as to be obliged to fell him-

E 6   felf.

felf*. This fuppofes a moderation of poffeffions and credit on the fide of the great, and the moderation of defires and covetoufnefs on the part of the little.

This equality, they tell us, is a mere fpeculative chimera, which cannot exift in practice: but though abufes are inevitable, does it thence follow they are not to be corrected? It is for the very reafon that things always tend to deftroy this equality, that the laws fhould be calculated to preferve it.

Thefe general objects of legiflature, however, fhould be varioufly modified in different countries, agreeable to local fituation, the character of the inhabitants, and thofe other circumftances which require that every people fhould have a particular fyftem of laws, not always the beft in itfelf, but the beft adapted to

* Would you give a ftate confiftency and ftrength, prevent the two extremes as much as poffible; let there be no rich perfons nor beggars. Thefe two conditions, naturally infeparable, are equally deftructive to the commonwealth: the one furnifhes tyrants, and the other the fupporters of tyranny. It is by thofe the traffic of public liberty is carried on; the one buying, the other felling it.

that

that ftate for which it is calculated. If, for example, the foil be ungrateful and barren, or the
country too fmall for its inhabitants, cherifh induftry and the arts, the productions of which
may be exchanged for the commodities required.
On the other hand, if your country abounds in
fertile hills and plenteous vales; if you live on
a rich foil in want of inhabitants; apply your-
felves to agriculture, which affords the means
of population ; and banifh the deftructive arts
which ferve only to ruin a country, by gather-
ing the few inhabitants of it, together in one particular fpot or two, to the depopulation of all
the reft *. Do you occupy an extenfive and
commodious fituation by the fea fide ? Cover the
ocean with your fhips, cultivate the arts of
navigation and commerce : you will by thefe
means enjoy a brilliant but fhort exiftence. On
the contrary, do the waves only wafte their
ftrength againft your inacceffible rocks ? Remain barbarous and illiterate ; you will live but
the more at eafe, perhaps more virtuous, af-

* The advantage of foreign commerce, fays the
Marquis d'A. is productive only of a delufive utility
to the kingdom in general. It may enrich a few individuals, and perhaps fome cities; but the whole
nation gains nothing by it, nor are the people the
better for it.

furedly

.furedly more happy. In a word, befides the maxims common to all nations, every people are poffeffed in themfelves of fome caufe which influences them in a particular manner, and renders their own fyftem of laws proper only .for themfelves. It is thus that in ancient times, among the Hebrews, and in modern times, a-mong the Arabians, religion was made the principal object of national concern; among the Athenians this object was literature; at Carthage and Tyre it was commerce, at Rhodes it was navigation, at Sparta war, and at Rome public virtue. The author of the *Spirit of laws* hath fhewn, by a number of examples, in what manner the legiflator fhould model his fyftem agreeable to each of thefe objects.

What renders the conftitution of a ftate truly folid and durable, is that agreement maintained therein between natural and focial relations, which occafions the legiflature always to act in concert with nature, while the laws ferve only to confirm and rectify, as it were, the dictates of the former. But if the legiflator, deceived in his object, fhould affume a principle different from that which arifes from the nature of things; fhould the one tend to flavery and the other to liberty, one to riches, the other to population,

one

one to peace the other to war and conquefts, the laws would infenfibly lofe their force, the conftitution would alter, and the ftate continue to be agitated till it fhould be totally changed or deftroyed, and nature have refumed its empire.

CHAP. XII.

On the divifion of the laws.

IN order to provide for the government of the whole, or give the beft poffible form to the conftitution, various circumftances are to be taken into confideration. Of thefe the firft is the action of the whole body operating on it-felf; that is the relation of the whole to the whole, or of the fovereign to the ftate, which relation is compofed of thofe between the intermediate terms; as will be feen hereafter.

The laws which govern this relation bear the name of politic laws, and are alfo called fundamental laws, not without fome reafon when they are wifely ordained. For if there be only one good method of government in a ftate, the peo-ple, who have been fo happy as to hit on that method, ought to abide by it: but, wherefore

4   fhould

should a people, whose laws are bad or defective, esteem such laws to be fundamental? Besides, a nation is in any case at liberty to change even the best laws, when it pleases: for if a people have a mind even to do themselves an injury, who hath any right to prevent them?

The second circumstance is the relations which the members of the community bear to each other and to the whole body, the first of which should be as little, and the last as great, as possible: so that every citizen should live in a state of perfect independence on all the rest, and in a state of the greatest dependence on the city. Both these are ever effected by the same means: for it is the power of the state only that constitutes the liberty of its members. On this second kind of relation is laid the immediate foundation of the civil laws.

It may be proper to consider also a third species of relation between the individual and the law; which gives immediate rise to penal statutes: these, however, are in fact less a distinct species of laws than the sanction of all the others.

To

To these three kinds of laws, may be added a fourth, more important than all the rest ; and which are neither engraven on brass or marble ; but in the hearts of the citizens ; forming the real constitution of the state. These are the laws which acquire daily fresh influence, and when others grow old and obsolete, invigorate and revive them : these are the laws which keep alive in the hearts of the people, the original spirit of their institution, and substitute insensibly the force of habit to that of authority. The laws I here speak of, are manners, customs, and above all public opinion ; all unknown or disregarded by our modern politicians, but on which depends the success of all the rest. These are the objects on which the real legislator is employed in secret, while he appears solely to confine himself to those particular regulations which compose only the preparatory centre of the vault, of which manners, more slow in their progress, form in the end the immoveable arch.

Of these classes, politic laws, or those which constitute the form of government, are relative only to my present subject.

The END of the SECOND BOOK.

BOOK

BOOK III.

BEFORE we enter on a difcuffion of the feveral forms of government, it will not be improper to afcertain the precife meaning of that term; which as yet hath not been well explained.

CHAP. I.

On government in general.

I MUST previoufly caution the reader to perufe this chapter very deliberately, as it is impoffible to render myfelf clearly intelligible to fuch as are not attentive.

Every free action hath two caufes, which concur to effect its production, the one moral, viz. the will which determines the act; the other phyfical, viz. the power which puts it in execution. When I walk, for inftance, toward any particular object, it is firft neceffary that I fhould will to go; and fecondly that my feet fhould bear me forward. A paralytic may will to run, and an active racer be unwilling; the want of power in the one hath the fame effect

as

as the want of will in the other; both remain in their place. The body politic hath the fame principles of motion; which are diftinguifhed alfo in the fame manner by power and will: the latter under the name of the *legiflative* power, and the former under that of the *executive* power. Nothing is or ought to be done without the concurrence of both.

We have already feen that the legiflative power belongs to the people in general, and can belong to none elfe. On the other hand, it is eafy to conclude, from the principles already eftablifhed, that the executive power cannot appertain to the generality, as legiflator or fovereign; becaufe this power is exerted only in particular acts which are not the province of the law, nor of courfe that of the fovereign, whofe acts can be no other than laws.

To the public force, therefore, fhould be annexed a proper agent, which may re-unite and put it in action, agreeable to the directions of the general will; ferving as a communication between the ftate and the fovereign, and effecting the fame purpofe in the body politic, as the union of the foul and body in man. Such is the rationale of government, fo generally confounded

founded with the fovereign, of which it is only the miniftry.

What then is government? It is an intermediate body eftablifhed between the fubject and the fovereign, for their mutual correfpondence; charged with the execution of the laws, and with the maintenance of civil and political liberty.

The members of which this body is compofed, are called magiftrates or *kings*, that is to fay, *governors*, and the whole body bears the name of the *prince* *. Thofe, therefore, who affirm that the act, by which a people profefs fubmiffion to their chiefs or governors, is not a contract, are certainly right; it being in fact nothing more than the conferring a fimple commiffion on the faid chiefs; an employ, in the difcharge of which they act as mere officers of the fovereign, exercifing in its name the power which it hath placed in their hands, and which it may limit, modify or refume whenever it pleafes; the alienation of its right fo to do, being incompatible with the very nature and being of fociety.

* Thus at Venice the college of ferators is called the moft ferene *prince*, even when the doge is not prefent.

I call

I call therefore, the legal exercife of the executive power, the *Government* or fupreme adminiftration; and the individual or body, charged with that adminiftration, the prince or the
magiftrate.

In the government are to be found thofe intermediate forces, whofe relations compofe that
of the whole to the whole, or of the fovereign
to the ftate.   This laft relation may be reprefented by that of the extremes of a conftant
proportion, the mean proportional of which is
the government.   The government receives from
the fovereign thofe orders, which it gives to the
people ; fo that, in order to keep the ftate in
due equilibrio, there fhould, every thing confidered, be the fame equality between the momentum or force of the government taken in
itfelf, and the momentum or force of the citizens, who are the fovereign confidered collectively on one fide, and fubjects confidered feverally
on the other.

It is, befides, impoffible to vary any of thefe
three terms, without inftantly deftroying the proportions.   If the fovereign fhould be defirous
to govern, or the magiftrate to give laws, or
the fubjects refufe to obey ; diforder muft im-
me-

mediately take place; the will and the power thus no longer acting in concert, the ftate would be diffolved, and fall into defpotifm or anarchy. Add to this, that as there can be but one mean proportional between each relation, there can be but one good government for a ftate. But as a thoufand events may change the relations fubfifting among a people; different governments may not only be good for different people, but even for the fame people at different periods of time.

In order to give the reader an idea of the various relations that may exift between thefe two extremes, I fhall, by way of example, make ufe of the number of people, as a relation the moft eafily expreffed.

We will fuppofe, for inftance, that a ftate is compofed of ten thoufand citizens. The fovereign muft be confidered as collectively only and in a body: but every particular in quality of fubject is confidered as an individual: thus the fovereign is in this cafe to the fubject as ten thoufand to one: That is to fay, every member of the ftate fhares only the ten thoufandth part of the fovereign authority; while at the fame time he is fubjected to it in his whole perfon. Again, fhould the number of people be increafed

to

to an hundred thoufand, the fubmiffion of the
fubjects would receive no alteration; each of
them being totally fubjected to the authority of
the laws, while his fhare in the fovereignty,
and vote in the enaction of thefe laws, would
be reduced to the hundred-thoufandth part; a
tenth lefs than before. Thus the fubject, remaining always a fingle integer, the proportion
between him and the fovereign increafes as the
number of citizens is augmented: whence it
follows, that as a ftate increafes, the liberty
of the fubject diminifhes.

When I fay the proportion increafes, I mean
that it recedes farther from the point of equality. Thus the greater the proportion, in the
language of the geometricians, it is reckoned
the lefs according to common acceptation: a-
greeable to the former, the relation, confidered
in point of quantity, is eftimated by its extent;
and according to the latter, confidered in point
of identity, it is eftimated by its proxima-
tion.

Now, the lefs proportion which particular
voices bear to the general, that is to fay, the
manners to the laws, the more ought the general reftrictive force to be augmented. Thus the
government fhould be relatively more powerful
as the people are more numerous.

On

On the other hand, the increasing greatness of a state affording the guardians of the public authority greater temptations and means to abuse their power, the more force a government is possessed of to restrain the people, the more ought the sovereign to be possessed of in its turn to restrain the government. I am not speaking here of absolute power, but of the relative forces of the component parts of the state.

It follows, from this two-fold relation, that the constant proportion between the sovereign, the prince, and the people, is not a mere arbitrary idea, but a necessary consequence of the very existence of the body politic. It follows also, that, one of the extremes, viz. the people as subjects, being a fixed term represented by unity, wherever the two-fold ratio is increased or diminished, that the simple ratio must increase or diminish in like manner, and of course the mean term will be changed. Hence it appears there is no one settled constitution of government, but that there may be as many governments different in their nature as there are states differing in magnitude.

If

If any one should affect to turn my system into ridicule, and say that, in order to find this mean proportional, and form the government as it ought to be, we have no more to do than to find the square root of the number of the people; I answer that I here make use of the number of people only by way of example; that the relations of which I have been speaking, are not only estimated by the number of individuals, but in general by the momentum or quantity of action, which arises from a combination of various causes; and though, in order to express myself concisely, I borrow the terms of geometry, I am not ignorant that geometrical precision is not to be expected in treating of moral quantities.

The government is in miniature what the body politic containing it, is at large. It is a moral person endued with certain faculties, active as the sovereign, passive as the state, and capable of being resolved into other sensible relations, from which of course arises a new scale of proportion, and still another within this, according to the order of the courts of justice, till we arrive at the last indivisible term, that is to say, the sole chief or supreme magistrate, which may be represented in the centre

F

of

of this progreſſion, as an unity between the
ſeries of fractions, and that of whole numbers.

But, without embarraſſing the reader with a
multiplicity of terms, we ſhall content ourſelves
with conſidering the government as a new body
in the ſtate, diſtinct from the ſubjects and the
ſovereign, and exiſting between both.

There is this eſſential difference, however,
between the government and the ſtate, that the
latter exiſts of itſelf, and the former only by
means of the ſovereign. Thus as the ruling
will of the prince is, or ought to be, only the
general will, or the law, the power of the
prince is only that of the public centered in
him; ſo that whenever he would derive from
himſelf any abſolute and independent act, the
combination of the whole is affected. And if,
at length, the prince ſhould have a particular
will of his own, more active than that of the
ſovereign, and ſhould make uſe of the public
power in his hands to enforce obedience to ſuch
particular will, forming, as it were, two ſovereigns, the one of right and the other of
fact, the ſocial union immediately vaniſhes, and
the body politic is diſſolved.

In

In order that the body of government, never-theless, may have an exiftence, a real life to diftin-guifh it from that of the ftate, and that its members may act in concert to anfwer the end for which it is inftituted, it is neceffary that it fhould be poffeffed of a particular identity, a fenfibility common to all its members, a power and will of its own for the fake of its prefervation.   Such a particular exiftence neceffarily fuppofes that of affemblies and councils ; of a power to de-liberate and refolve ; of the rights, titles and privileges which belong exclufively to the prince, and render the fituation of a magiftrate the more honourable in proportion as it is more laborious.   The difficulty lies in the me-thod of difpofing all the inferior parts of the whole body ; fo that, while it is ftrengthening its own conftitution, it may not injure that of the ftate.   At the fame time alfo, it fhould always diftinguifh between the peculiar force, deftined to its own prefervation, and the public force deftined to the prefervation of the ftate ; in a word, it fhould be always ready to facri-fice the government to the people, and not the people to the government.

To this we may add, that, although the ar-tificial body of government be the work of an-

F 2   other

other artificial body, and is poſſeſſed only of a borrowed and ſubordinate exiſtence ; this doth not prevent it from acting with different degrees of vigour and celerity, or from enjoying, if I may ſo expreſs myſelf, a greater or leſs ſhare of health and ſtrength. In ſhort, it may, without running diametrically oppoſite to the purpoſes of its inſtitution, deviate from them more or leſs, according to the mode in which it is conſtituted.

It is from all theſe differences that ariſe thoſe various relations and proportions, which the government ought to bear toward the ſtate, according to theſe accidental and particular relations in which the ſtate is modified. For the beſt government in itſelf may often become the worſt, if the relation of its component parts are not altered according to the defects of the body politic to which it belongs.

CHAP.

CHAP. II.

On the principle which conftitutes the different forms of government.

TO explain the general caufe of thefe dif-ferences, it is neceffary to diftinguifh here between the prince and the government, in the fame manner as I have already done between the fovereign and the ftate. The body of the magiftracy may be compofed of a greater or a lefs number of members. It hath been obferved alfo that the relation the fovereign bears to the fubject increafes in proportion to the num-ber of people ; thus, by an evident analogy, we may fay the fame of the relation between the government and the magiftrates.

Now the total force of the government, being always equal to that of the ftate, fuffers no al-teration ; whence it follows that the more fuch force is fpent by the diftribution of it among the members of the government, the lefs re-mains to be exerted on the whole body of people.

F 3

That

That government, therefore, which is in the hands of the greatest number of magistrates must be the most feeble. As this is a fundamental maxim, we shall take some pains to illustrate it.

In the person of the magistrate may be distinguished three wills essentially different. In the first place the particular will of the individual, which tends only to his private advantage; secondly, that will which is common to him as a magistrate, tending solely to the advantage of the prince; being general with respect to the government, and particular with regard to the state, of which the government is only a part; and in the third place, the will of the people or the sovereign will, which is general as well with regard to the state considered as a whole, as with regard to the government considered as a part of that whole.

In a compleat system of legislature, the particular will or that of the individual should amount to nothing; the will of the body of government should be very limited, and of course the general or sovereign will the ruling and sole director of all the others.

Ac-

According to the order of nature, however, thefe different wills are ranged in a contrary manner; being always more active as they are concentrated in themfelves. Thus the general will is always the moft feeble, that of the government next, and the will of the individual the ftrongeft of all; fo that each member of the adminiftration is to be confidered firft of all as an individual, fecondly as a magiftrate, and laftly as a citizen: a gradation directly oppofite to that which the order of fociety requires.

This point being fettled, let us fuppofe the adminiftration of government committed to the hands of one man. In this cafe the will of the individual, and that of the body of the magiftracy are perfectly united, and of confequence the latter poffeffes the greateft degree of intenfity. Now, as it is on the degree of the will that the exertion of force depends, and as the abfolute force of the government never varies, it follows that the moft active of all adminiftrations muft be that of a fingle perfon.

On the contrary, if we unite the adminiftration and the legiflature; if we make the prince

F 4

the

the fovereign, and the citizens all fo many magiftrates: in this cafe, the will of the government, confounded with the general will, would
poffefs no greater fhare of activity, but would
leave the particular will of individuals to exert
its whole force. Thus the government, having always the fame degree of abfolute force,
would be at its *minimum* of relative force or
activity.

Thefe relations are inconteftible, and may be
farther confirmed by other confiderations. It
is evident, for example, that the magiftrate is
more active in that capacity than the citizen in
his, and that of courfe the will of the individual muft have a more confiderable fhare of influence in the adminiftration of government,
than in the actions of the fovereign; every
magiftrate being almoft always charged with
fome function of government, whereas no ci-.
tizen, confidered as an individual, difcharges
any function of the fovereignty. Befide this,
the real force of a ftate increafes, as the ftate
increafes in magnitude, though not always in
the ratio of that magnitude; but while the
ftate remains the fame, it is in vain to increafe
the number of magiftrates, as the government
will not thereby acquire any additional ftrength,

becaufe

becaufe its force, being always. that of the ftate, is conftantly equal. And thus the relative force or activity of government is diminifh-ed, without its real and abfolute force being augmented.

It is farther certain that public affairs muft be tranfacted more or lefs expeditioufly according to the number of people, charged with their difpatch; that by laying too great a ftrefs on prudence, too little is trufted to fortune; that the opportunity of fuccefs is thus frequently loft, and that by the mere force of deliberation: the end of. it is defeated.

This may ferve to prove that the reins of government are relaxed in proportion as the magiftrates are multiplied; and I have before demonftrated that the more numerous the people are, the more fhould the reftraining power of government be increafed: Hence it follows that the proportion which the number of magiftrates fhould hold to the government fhould be in the inverfe ratio of the fubjects to the fovereign; that is to fay, the more extenfive the ftate the more contracted fhould be the government, the number of chiefs diminifhing as that of the people increafes.

F 5. I. fpeak

I fpeak here only of the relative force of the government, and not of the rectitude or propriety of it. For, otherwife, it is certain that the more numerous the magiftracy is, the nearer doth the will of that body approach to the general will of the whole people; whereas under a fole chief, the will of the magiftracy is, as I have before obferved, only that of an individual. Thus what is gained in one refpect, is loft on the other; and the art of the legiflator confifts in tracing the fixed point, at which the force and the will of the government, always in a reciprocal proportion to each other, unite in that proportion which is moft advantageous to the ftate.

C H A P. III.

Of the actual diftinctions of governments.

WE have treated in the preceding chapter of the reafons for diftinguifhing the feveral fpecies and forms of government, by the number of the members compofing them; it remains therefore to fhew, in the prefent, how thefe diftinctions are actually made.

The

The fovereign authority may, in the firſt place, commit the charge of the government to the whole people or to the greater paſt of them ; the number of magiſtrates in ſuch caſe exceeding that of private citizens. This form of government is diſtinguiſhed by the name of a democracy.

Or, otherwiſe, the ſupreme power may commit the office of government into the hands of a few, ſo that the number of private citizens may exceed that of magiſtrates ; and this form bears the name of an ariſtocracy.

Or laſtly, the government may be entruſted to one magiſtrate only, who delegates his power to all the reſt. This third form is the moſt common, and is called a monarchy or a regal government.

It is to be obſerved that all theſe forms, and particularly the two former, are ſuſceptible of different degrees of perfection, and admit indeed of conſiderable latitude in their modification : for a democracy may comprehend the whole people, or be limited to the half. An ariſtocracy alſo may comprehend any quantity

from

from the half of the people to the smallest
number indefinitely. Nay a monarchy itself is
susceptible of some distribution. Sparta, for
instance, had constitutionally two kings at a
time; and the Romans had even eight emperors
at once, without the empire having been actually divided. Thus, we see, there is a certain point, at which each form of government
is confounded with that to which it is nearest re-
lated; and thus under three distinguishing de-
nominations only, government is really susceptible of as many different forms, as there are
citizens in the state.

To go still farther; as even one and the same
government is capable, in many respects, of being
subdivided into parts, of which the administration may respectively differ, there may result
from the varied combinations of these forms a
multitude of others, every one of which may
be again multiplied by all the simple forms.

Politicians have in all ages disputed much
about the best form of government, without
considering that each different form may pos-
sibly be the best in some cases, and the worst in
others.

If

If in different states the number of supreme magistrates should be in the inverse ratio to that of the citizens, it follows that the democratical government is generally speaking better suited to small states, the aristocratical to middling states, and the monarchical to great states. This rule is deduced immediately from our principles; but it is impossible to particularize the multiplicity of circumstances which may furnish exceptions against it.

CHAP. IV.

Of a Democracy.

THE institutor of a law should certainly know better than any other person, how it ought to be understood and executed. It should seem therefore that the best constitution, must be that in which the legislative and executive powers are lodged in the same hands. It is this very circumstance, however, that renders such a government imperfect; because there doth not exist the necessary distinction, which ought to be made in its parts; while the prince and the sovereign, being one and the same person, only form, if I may so express myself, a government without a government.

It

It is not proper that the power which makes
the laws ſhould execute them, or that the attention of the whole body of the people ſhould
be diverted from general views to particular objects.   Nothing is more dangerous than the influence of private intereſt in publick affairs;
the abuſe of the laws by the government, being
a leſs evil than the corruption of the legiſlature;
which is infallibly the conſequence of its being
governed by particular views.   For in that caſe,
the ſtate being eſſentially altered, all reformation
becomes impoſſible.   A people who would not
abuſe the power of government, would be no
more propenſe to abuſe their independence; and
a people who ſhould always govern well, would
have no occaſion to be governed at all.

To take the term in its ſtricteſt ſenſe, there
never exiſted, and never will exiſt, a real democracy in the world.   It is contrary to the
natural order of things, that the majority of a
people ſhould be the governors, and the minority the governed.   It is not to be conceived
that a whole people ſhould remain perſonally
aſſembled to manage the affairs of the public;
and it is evident, that no ſooner are deputies or
repreſentatives appointed, than the form of the
adminiſtration is changed.

It

It may be laid down indeed as a maxim, that when the functions of government are divided among several courts, that which is composed of the fewest persons will, sooner or later, acquire the greatest authority; though it were for no other reason than the facility with which it is calculated to expedite affairs.

Such a form of government suppofes, also, the concurrence of a number of circumstances rarely united. In the first place, it is requisite that the state itself should be of small extent, so that the people might be easily assembled and all personally known to each other. Secondly, the simplicity of their manners should be such as to prevent a multiplicity of affairs, and perplexity in discussing them : And thirdly, there should subsist a great degree of equality between the rank and fortunes of individuals; without which there cannot exist long any equality between them in point of right and authority. Lastly, there should be little or no luxury; for luxury must either be the effect of wealth, or it must make it necessary; it corrupts at once both rich and poor; the one by means of the possession of wealth, and the other by means of the want of it. Luxury makes a sacrifice of

pa-

patriotifm to indolence and vanity; it robs a ftate of its citizens by fubjecting them to each other, and by fubjecting all to the influence of public prejudice.

It is for this reafon that a certain celebrated author hath laid down virtue as the firft principle of a republican government : for all thefe circumftances cannot concur without the exiftence of public virtue. For want, however, of making proper diftinctions, this great genius hath been led into frequent miftakes, as well as want of precifion ; not having obferved that, the fovereign authority being every where the fame, the fame principle muft take place in every well conftituted ftate ; though it is true in a greater or lefs degree, according to the form of government.

To this it may be added, that no government is fo fubject to civil wars and inteftine commotions as that of the democratical or popular form ; becaufe no other tends fo ftrongly and fo conftantly to alter, nor requires fo much vigilance and fortitude to preferve it from alteration. It is, indeed, in fuch a conftitution particularly that the citizen fhould always be armed.

ed with force and conftancy, and fhould repeat every day, in the fincerity of his heart, the faying of the virtuous palatine *. *Malo periculofam libertatem quam quietum fervitium.*

Did there exift a nation of Gods, their government would doubtlefs be democratical; it is too perfeft a form, however, for mankind.

CHAP. V.

Of an Arifloracy.

IN this form of government exift two moral perfons, very palpably diftinft, viz. the adminiftration and the fovereign; which of courfe poffefs two general wills, the one regarding the citizens univerfally; the other only the members of the adminiftration. Thus, although the government may regulate the interior police of the ftate as it pleafes, it cannot addrefs the people but in the name of the fovereign, that is to fay, the people themfelves; which is a circumftance never to be omitted. The primitive focieties of mankind were governed ariftocrati-

* The Palatine of Pofnania, father of the king of Poland, Duke of Lorrain.

cally.

cally. The heads of families deliberated among themfelves concerning public affairs; the young people readily fubmitting to the authority of experience. Hence the names of *Priefts*, the *Fathers*, the *Senate*, &c. The favages of North America are governed in the fame manner to this day, and are extremely well governed.

But, in proportion as the inequality arifing from focial inftitutions prevailed over natural inequality, riches and power were preferred to age *, and the ariftocracy became elective. At length power, tranfmitted with property from father to fon, making whole families patrician, rendered the government hereditary, and boys of twenty became fenators.

Ariftocracy therefore is of three kinds; natural, elective and hereditary. The firft, is applicable only to the moft fimple ftate of fociety, while the laft is the worft of all kinds of government. The fecond is the beft ; and is what is moft properly denominated an ariftocracy.

---

* It is evident that the term *optimates* among the ancients, did not mean the beft, but moft powerful.

Beſide the advantage of the abovementioned diſtinction, this form hath alſo that of the choice of its members: in a popular government all the citizens are born magiſtrates; but in this the number of the latter are very limited, and they become ſuch only by election *; a method by which their probity, their talents, their experience, and all thoſe other reaſons for preference in the public eſteem, are an additional ſecurity that the people ſhall be wiſely governed.

Again, their public aſſemblies are attended with more decorum; affairs of ſtate are more regularly diſcuſſed, and buſineſs executed with greater order and expedition; while the credit of the ſtate is better ſupported, in the eyes of foreigners, by a ſelect number of venerable ſenators, than by a promiſcuous or contemptible mob.

* It is of great importance to regulate by law the method of chuſing magiſtrates; for, in leaving this to the prince, it is impoſſible to avoid falling into an hereditary ariſtocracy, as happened to the republics of Venice and Berne. Hence the firſt has been long ſince diſſolved, but the ſecond hath been ſupported by the great prudence of the Senate. This is an exception, however, as dangerous as honourable.

In

In a word, that order would be undoubtedly the best and most natural, according to which the wise and experienced few direct the multitude, were it certain that the few would in their government consult the interest of the majority governed, and not their own. It is absurd to multiply the springs of action to no purpose, or to employ twenty thousand men in doing that, which an hundred properly selected would effect much better.

With regard to the particular circumstances requisite to this form of government; the state should not be so small, nor the manners of the people so simple or so virtuous as that the execution of the laws should coincide with the public Will, as in a well founded democracy. On the other hand also, the state should not be so extensive that the governors, distributed up and down its provinces, might be able to render themselves, each in his separate department, independant of the sovereign.

But if an aristocracy requires fewer virtues than a popular government; there are yet some which are peculiar to it; such as moderation in the rich and content in the poor : an exact equality

lity of condition would in fuch a government be quite improper : nor was it obferved even at Sparta.

If a certain degree however, of inequality in the fortunes of the people, be proper in fuch a government; the reafon of it is, that in general the adminiftration of public affairs, ought to be put into the hands of thofe perfons who can beft devote their time to fuch fervice; not, as Ariftotle pretends, that the rich ought always to be preferred merely on account of their wealth. On the contrary, it is very neceffary that an oppofite choice fhould fometimes teach the people that there exift other motives of preference much more important than riches.

CHAP. VI.

On monarchy.

HITHERTO we have confidered the prince as a moral and collective perfonage, formed by the force of the laws, and as the depofitory of the executive power of the ftate. At prefent, it is our bufinefs to confider this power, as lodged in the hands of a phyfical perfonage or real man; poffeffed of the right of ex-

exerting it agreeable to the laws.   Such a perfon is denominated a monarch or king.

In other adminiftrations it is common for a
collective body to reprefent an individual being ;
whereas in this an individual is, on the contrary, the reprefentative of a collective body;
fo that the moral unity which conftitutes the
prince, is at the fame time a phyfical unity, in
which all the faculties which the law combines
in the former are combined naturally in the
latter.

Thus the will of the people and that of the
prince, together with the public force of the
ftate, and the particular force of the government, all depend on the fame principle of action :
all the fprings of the machine are in the fame
hand, are exerted to the fame end ; there are no
oppofite motions counteracting and deftroying
each other ; nor is it poffible to conceive any
fpecies of government in which the leaft effort
is productive of fo great a quantity of action.
Archimedes, fitting at his eafe on the fhore,
and moving about a large veffel on the ocean
at pleafure, reprefents to my imagination an-able
monarch fitting in his cabinet, and governing
his diftant provinces, by keeping every thing in
motion,

motion, while he himself seems immoveable. But, if no other kind of government hath so much activity, there is none in which the particular will of the individual is so predominant. Every thing, it is true, proceeds toward the same end ; but this end is not that of public happiness ; and hence the force of the administration operates inceffantly to the prejudice of the state.

Kings would be absolute, and they are sometimes told that their best way to become so, is to make themselves beloved by the people. This maxim is doubtless a very fine one, and even in some respects true. But unhappily it is laughed at in courts. That power which arises from the love of the people is without doubt the greatest : but it is so precarious and conditional, that princes have never been satisfied with it. Even the best kings are desirous of having it in their power to do ill when they please, without losing their prerogatives. It is to no purpose that a declaiming politician tells them that the strength of the people being theirs, it is their greatest interest to have the people flourishing, numerous and respectable : they know that this is not true. Their personal and private interest

is,

is, in the firft place, that the people fhould be
fo weak and miferable as to be incapable of making any refiftance to government. I confefs
indeed that, fuppofing the people to be held in
perfeƈt fubjeƈtion, it would be to the intereft
of the prince that they fhould be rich and
powerful, becaufe their ftrength, being alfo
his, ferves to make him refpeƈtable to his neighbours; but as this intereft is only fecondary
and fubordinate, and that thefe fuppofitions are
incompatible, it is natural for princes to give
the preference always to that maxim which is
the moft immediately ufeful. This is what
Samuel hath reprefented very forcibly to the
Hebrews; and Machiavel hath made evident to a
demonftration. In affeƈting to give inftruƈtions
to kings, he hath given the moft ftriking leffons
to the people: His book entitled the Prince, is
particularly adapted to the fervice of Republics.

We have already fhewn from the general relations of things, that a monarchy is fuitable only
to great ftates, and we fhall be more particularly
convinced of it, on a further examination. The
more numerous the members of the public adminiftration, the more is the relation beween
the prince and the fubjeƈts diminifhed, and the
nearer

nearer it approaches to nothing, or that point of
equality which fubfifts in a democracy. This
relation increafes in proportion as the government
is contracted; and arrives at its *maximum* when
the adminiftration is in the hands of a fingle
perfon. In this cafe, then, there is too great
a diftance between the prince and people, and
the ftate is void of connection. To fupply its
place, therefore, recourfe is had to the intermediate ranks of people. Hence the feveral
orders of nobility. But nothing of this kind
is fuitable to a fmall ftate, to which thefe different ranks are very deftructive.

If the good government of a ftate be a matter of difficulty under any mode of adminiftration, it is more particularly fo in the hands of
a fingle perfon; and every body knows the
confequences when a king reigns by fubftitutes.

Again, there is one effential and unavoidable
defect, which will ever render a monarchical government inferior to a republic; and this is, that
in the latter, the public voice hardly ever raifes
unworthy perfons to high pofts in the adminiftration; making choice only of men of knowlege and abilities, who difcharge their refpective

G   functions

functions with honour: whereas those who generally make their way to such posts under a monarchical government, are men of little minds and mean talents, who owe their preferment to the meritricious arts of flattery and intrigue. The public are less apt to be deceived in their choice than the prince; and a man of real merit is as rarely to be found in the ministry of a king, as a blockhead at the head of a republic. Thus, when by any fortunate accident, a genius born for government, takes the lead in a monarchy, brought to the verge of ruin by such petty rulers, the world is amazed at the resources he discovers, and his administration stands as a singular epoch in the history of his country.

To have a monarchical state well governed, it is requisite that its magnitude or extent should be proportioned to the abilities of the regent. It is more easy to conquer than to govern. By means of a lever sufficiently long, it were possible with a single finger to move the globe; but to support it requires the shoulders of an Hercules. When a state may with any propriety be denominated great, the prince is almost always too little. And when, on the contrary, it happens, which however is very seldom, that

that the ftate is too little for its regent, it
muft be ever ill-governed; becaufe the chief,
actuated by the greatnefs of his own ideas, is
apt to forget the intereft of his people, and
makes them no lefs unhappy from the abufe of
his fuperfluous talents, than would another of a
more limited capacity, for want of thofe talents
which fhould be neceffary. It is thence requifite, that a kingdom fhould, if I may fo fay,
contract and dilate itfelf, on every fucceffion,
according to the capacity of the reigning prince:
whereas the abilities of a fenate being more fixt,
the ftate, under a republican government, may
be confined or extended to any determinate limits, and the adminiftration be equally good.
The moft palpable inconvenience in the government of a fole magiftrate, is the default of
that continued fucceffion, which, in the two
other kinds, forms an uninterrupted connection
in the ftate. When one king dies, it is neceffary
to have another; but when kings are elective,
fuch elections form very turbulent and dangerous intervals; and unlefs the citizens are poffeffed of a difintereftednefs and integrity, incompatible with this mode of government, ve-
nality and corruption will neceffarily have an
influence over them. It is very rare that he,

to

to whom the ftate is fold, does not fell it again in his turn, and make the weak repay him the money extorted from him by the ftrong.   Every one becomes, fooner or later, venal and corrupt, under fuch an adminiftration ; while even the tranquillity, which is enjoyed under the kings, is worfe than the diforder attending their *inter-regnum.*

To remedy thefe evils, crowns have been made hereditary, and an order of fucceffion hath been eftablifhed, which prevents any difputes on the death of kings : that is to fay, by fub-ftituting the inconvenience of regencies to that of elections, an apparent tranquillity is preferred to a wife adminiftration ; and it is thought bet-ter to run the rifk of having the throne fup-plied by children, monfters, and ideots, than to have any difpute about the choice of good kings.   It is not confidered, that in expofing a ftate to the rifk of fuch an alternative, almoft every chance is againft it.

Almoft every thing confpires to deprive a youth, educated to the command over others, of the principles of reafon and juftice.   Great pains, it is faid, are taken to teach young princes the art

of

of reigning; it does not appear however that they profit much by their education. It would be better to begin by teaching them subjection. The greatest monarchs that have been celebrated in history, are those who were not educated to govern. This is a science of which those know the least who have been taught the most, and is better acquired by studying obedience than command. *Nam utilliſſimus idem ac breviſſimus bonarum malarumque rerum delectus, cogitare quid aut nolueris ſub alio principe aut volueris.*

A consequence of this want of coherence, is the inconſtancy of regal government, which is sometimes purſued on one plan, and sometimes on another, according to the character of the prince who governs, or of those who hold the reins of adminiſtration for him; ſo that its conduct is as inconſiſtent as the object of its purſuit is wavering. It is this inconſtancy which keeps the ſtate ever fluctuating from maxim to maxim, and from project to project; an uncertainty which does not take place in other kinds of government, where the prince is always the fame. Thus we ſee, in general, that if there be more cunning in a court, there is more true

wiſdom

wifdom in a fenate; and that republics accomplifh their ends, by means more conftant and
better purfued: while on the contrary, every
revolution in the miniftry of a court, produces
one in the ftate: it being the conftant máxim
with all minifters, and almoft with all kings,
to engage in meafures directly oppofite to thofe
of their immediate predeceffors. Again, it is
from this very incoherence that we may deduce
the folution of a fophifm very common with
regal politicians; and this is not only the practice of comparing the civil government of fociety to the domeftic government of a family,
and the prince to the father of it, (an error
already expofed) but alfo that of liberally be-
ftowing on the reigning magiftrate all the virtues
he ftands in need of, and of fuppofing the
prince always fuch as he ought to be. With
the help of this fuppofition, indeed, the regal
government is evidently preferable to all others,
becaufe it is inconteftably the ftrongeft; and nothing more is required to make it alfo the beft,
than that the will of the prince fhould be conformable to the general will of the people.

But if, according to Plato, the king by nature is fo very rare a perfonage, how feldom
may we fuppofe nature and fortune hath
concurred to crown him? If a regal education
also

alfo neceffarily corrupts thofe who receive it, what hopes can we have from a race of men thus educated? It is a wilful error, therefore, to confound a regal government in general with the government of a good king. But, to fee what this fpecies of government is in itfelf, it muft be confidered under the direction of weak and wicked princes: for fuch they generally are when they come to the throne, or fuch the throne will make them. Thefe difficulties have not efcaped the notice of fome writers, but they do not feem to have been much embarraffed by them. The remedy, fay they, is to obey without murmuring. God fends us bad things in his wrath, and we ought to bear with them as chaftifements from on high. This way of talk is certainly very edifying; but I conceive it would come with greater propriety from the pulpit, than from the pen of a politician. What fhould we fay of a phyfician who might promife miracles, and whofe whole art fhould confift in preaching up patience and refignation? It is obvious enough that we muft bear with a bad government, when we live under it; the queftion is to find a good one.

G 4   C H A P.

CHAP. VII.

Of mixed Governments.

THERE is no such thing, properly speaking, as a simple government. Even a sole chief must have inferior magistrates, and a popular government a chief. Thus in the distribution of the executive power there is always a gradation from the greater number to the less, with this difference that sometimes the greater number depends on the less, and at others the less on the greater.

Sometimes indeed the distribution is equal, either when the constituent parts depend mutually on each other, as in the English government; or when the authority of each part is independent, though imperfect, as in Poland. This last form is a bad one, because there is no union in such a government, and the several parts of the state want a due connection.

It is a question much agitated by politicians; Which is best, a simple or mixt government? The same answer however might be given to it,

as

as I have before made to the like queſtion concerning the forms of government in general.

A ſimple government is the beſt in itſelf,
though for no other reaſon than that it is ſimple.
But when the executive power is not ſufficiently
dependent on the legiſlative, that is to ſay, when
there is a greater diſproportion between the
prince and the ſovereign, than between the people and the prince, this defect muſt be remedied
by dividing the government; in which caſe all
its parts would have no leſs authority over the
ſubject, and yet their diviſion would render
them collectively leſs powerful to oppoſe their
ſovereign.

The ſame inconvenience is prevented alſo by
eſtabliſhing a number of inferior magiſtrates,
which tend to preſerve a ballance between the
two powers, and to maintain their reſpective
prerogatives. In this caſe, however, the government is not properly of a mixt kind; it is
only moderated.

The like means may alſo be employed to remedy an oppoſite inconvenience, as when a government is too feeble, by erecting of proper

tribunals

tribunals to concentrate its force. This method is practifed in all democracies. In the firft cafe, the adminiftration is divided in order to weaken it, and in the fecond to enforce it : For a *maximum* both of ftrength and weaknefs, is equally common to fimple governments, while thofe of mixt forms always give a mean proportional to both.

C H A P. VIII.

That every form of government is not equally proper for every country.

AS liberty is not the produce of all climates, fo it is not alike attainable by all people. The more one reflects on this principle, eftablifhed by Montefquieu, the more fenfible we become of its truth. The more it is contefted, the more we find it confirmed by new proofs.

Under every kind of government, the political perfonage, the public, confumes much, but produces nothing. Whence then doth it derive the fubftance confumed? Evidently from the labour of its members. It is from the fuperfluity of individuals that the neceffities of the public are provided. Hence it follows
that

that a focial ftate cannot fubfift longer than the induftry of its members continues to produce fuch fuperfluity.

The quantity of this fuperfluity, however, is not the fame in all countries. It is in many very confiderable, in fome but moderate, in others null, and again in others negative. The proportion depends on the fertility of the climate, the fpecies of labour required in the cultivation of the foil, the nature of its produce, the ftrength of its inhabitants, the confumption neceffary to their fubfiftence, with many other fimilar circumftances.

On the other hand, all governments are not of the fame nature; fome devour much more than others, and their difference is founded on this principle, viz. that the farther public contributions are removed from their fource, the more burthenfome they grow. It is not by the quantity of the impofition that we are to eftimate the burthen of it, but by the time or fpace taken up in its returning back to the hands, from which it is exacted. When this return is quick and eafy, it matters little whether fuch impofition be fmall or great; the people are

G 6 al-

always rich, and the finances in good condition. On the contrary, however low a people be taxed, if the money never returns, they are fure by conftantly paying to be foon exhaufted; fuch a ftate can never be rich, and the individuals of it muft be always beggars.

It follows hence that the farther the people are removed from the feat of government, the more burthenfome are their taxes: thus in a democracy their weight is leaft felt: in an ariftocracy they fall more heavy; and in a monarchical ftate they have the greateft weight of all. Monarchy, therefore, is proper only for opulent nations; ariftocracy for middling ftates; and a democracy for thofe which are mean and poor.

In faɛt, the more we refleɛt on this circumftance, the more plainly we perceive the difference in this refpeɛt between a monarchical and a free ftate. In the latter, all its force is ex   for the public utility; in the former, the public intereft of the ftate and the private intereft of the prince are reciprocally oppofed; the one increafing by the decreafe of the other.

In

In a word, inſtead of governing ſubjects in ſuch a manner as to make them happy, deſpotiſm makes them miſerable, in order to be able to govern them at all.

Thus may we trace in every climate thoſe natural cauſes, which point out that particular form of government which is beſt adapted to it, as well as even the peculiar kind of people that ſhould inhabit it. Barren and ungrateful ſoils, whoſe produce will not pay for the labour of cultivation, would remain uncultivated and uninhabited, or, at beſt, would be peopled only with ſavages. Thoſe countries from which the inhabitants might draw the neceſſaries of life, and no more, would be peopled by barbarians, among whom the eſtabliſhment of civil polity would be impoſſible. Such places as might yield to their inhabitants a moderate ſuperfluity, would be beſt adapted to a free people; while the country where fertile plains and plenteous vales more bounteouſly reward the labours of the cultivator, would beſt ſuit with a monarchical form of government, in order that the luxury of the prince might conſume the ſuperfluity of the ſubjects: for it is much better that this ſuperfluity ſhould be expended by government than diſſipated by individuals. I am not inſenſible that ſome exceptions

7

ceptions might be made to what is here advanced; thefe very exceptions, however, ferve
to confirm the general rule, in that they are
fooner or later conftantly productive of revolutions, which reduce things to their natural
order,

We fhould always make a diftinction between
general laws, and thofe particular caufes which
may diverfify their effects. For, though the
fouthern climates fhould be actually filled with
republics, and the northern with defpotic
monarchies, it would be neverthelefs true in
theory, that, fo far as climate is concerned, defpotifm agrees beft with an hot, barbarifm with
a cold, and good polity with a temperate re-
gion. I am aware farther that, even granting
the principle, the application of it may be dif-
puted. It may be faid, that fome cold countries are very fertile, while others more warm
and fouthern are very barren. This objection,
however, hath weight only with fuch as do not
examine the matter in every point of view. It
is requifite to take into confideration, as I before obferved, the labour of the people, their
ftrength, their confumption, with every other
circumftance that affects the point in queftion.

Let

Let us suppose two countries of equal extent, the proportion of whose product should be as five to ten. It is plain that, if the inhabitants of the first consume four, and of the latter nine, the superfluity of the one would be $\frac{1}{5}$, and that of the other $\frac{1}{5}$. Their different superfluities being also in an inverse ratio to that of their produce, the territory whose produce should amount only to five, would have near double the superfluity of that which should amount to ten.

But the argument does not rest upon a double produce; nay I doubt whether any person will place the actual fertility of cold countries in general, in a bare equality with that of warmer climates. We will suppose them, however, to be in this respect simply equal; setting England, for instance, on a balance with Sicily, and Poland with Egypt. Still farther to the South we have Africa and the Indies, and to the North hardly any thing. But to effect this equality in the produce, what a difference in the labour of cultivation! In Sicily they have nothing more to do than barely turn up the earth: in England agriculture is extremely toilsome and laborious. Now, where a greater number of hands

hands is required to raife the fame produce, the fuperfluity muft neceffarily be lefs.

Add to this, that the fame number of people confume much lefs in a warm country than in a cold one. An hot climate requires men to be temperate, if they would preferve their health. Of this the Europeans are made fenfible, by feeing thofe who do not alter their manner of living in hot countries, daily carried off by dyfenteries and indigeftion. Chardin reprefents us, as beafts of prey, as mere wolves in comparifon of the Afiatics; and thinks thofe writers miftaken, who have attributed the temperance of the Perfians, to the uncultivated ftate of their country. His opinion is that their country was fo little cultivated, becaufe the inhabitants required fo little for their fubfiftence. If their frugality were merely the effect of the barrennefs of their country, he obferves, it would be only the poorer fort of them that fhould eat little; whereas their abftinence is general. Again, they would in fuch cafe be more or lefs abftemious in different provinces, as thofe provinces differed in degrees of fterility; whereas their fobriety is general, and prevails equally throughout the kingdom. He tells us,

us, alfo, that the Perfians boaft much of their
manner of living ; pretending their complexions
only to be a fufficient indication, of its being
preferable to that of the Chriftians. At the
fame time, he admits that their complexions
are very fine and fmooth ; that their fkin is of
a foft texture, and polifhed appearance;
while, on the other hand, the complexion of
the Armenians, their fubjects, who live after
the European manner, is rough and pimply,
and their bodies grofs and unwieldy.

The nearer we approach to the line, it is
certain, the more abftemious we find the people. They hardly ever eat meat ; rice and maize
are their ordinary food. There are millions of
people in the Indies, whofe fubfiftence does not
amount to the value of a penny a day. We
fee even in Europe, a very fenfible difference,
in this refpect, between the inhabitants of the
North and South. A Spaniard will fubfift a
whole week, on what a German would eat up
at a fingle meal. In countries where the people are voracious, even luxury hath a tendency
to confumption. Thus in England it difplays
itfelf in the number of difhes and quantity of
folid meat on the table ; while in Italy, a re-
paft

paſt is furniſhed out with ſweetmeats and
flowers.

The luxury of dreſs preſents us, alſo, with
ſimilar differences. In climates, where the
change of the weather is ſudden and violent,
the people wear better and plainer clothes;
while in thoſe where the inhabitants dreſs only
for ornament, brilliancy is more conſulted than
uſe; even clothes themſelves are an article of
luxury. Thus at Naples, you will daily ſee
gentlemen walking about in laced clothes without ſtockings. It is the ſame with regard to
buildings : magnificence only is conſulted, where
nothing is to be feared from the inclemencies of
the weather. At Paris and London people are
deſirous of warm and commodious apartments.
At Madrid, they have ſuperb ſaloons, but no
ſaſhes nor caſements; and their beds lie open
to the rats that harbour in the roof.

The aliment is alſo more ſubſtantial and nou-
riſhing in hot countries than in cold ; this is a third
difference that cannot fail to have an influence
over the ſecond. Wherefore is it that the Italians
eat ſuch a quantity of vegetables ? Becauſe they
are good, and of an excellent ſavour. In France,
where

where they are themselves nourished chiefly by water, they are less nutritive, and are held of little consequence. They occupy nevertheless as much ground, and cost as much pains to cultivate them. It hath been experimentally proved that the corn of Barbary, in other respects inferior to that of France, gives a greater quantity of meal, and that the French corn yields still more than that of the North. Hence it may be inferred that a similar gradation is carried on in the same direction from the line to the pole. Now is it not an evident disadvantage to have, in an equal produce, a less quantity of aliment ?

To all these different considerations, I may add another, which arises from, and serves to confirm them; this is, that hot countries require fewer inhabitants than the cold, and yet afford subsistence for more ; a circumstance that causes a two-fold superfluity, always to the advantage of despotism. The more the same number of people are distributed over the face of a large territory, the more difficult becomes a revolt ; as they cannot meet together so readily or secretly, and it is always easy for the government to cut off their associations, and ruin their projects.

jects. On the other hand, the more a numerous people are collected together, the lefs can
the government affume over the fovereign; the
chiefs of a faction may deliberate as fecurely
at their meetings, as the prince in his council;
and the mob are as readily affembled in the
public fquares as the troops in their quarters.
It is the advantage of a tyrannical government,
therefore, to act at great diftances; its force
increafing with the diftance like that of a lever *,
by the affiftance of a proper center. That of
the people, on the contrary, acts only by being
concentrated; it evaporates and lofes itfelf when
dilated, even as gunpowder fcattered on the
ground, takes fire, particle by particle, and is
productive of no effect. Countries thinly in-

* This doth not contradict what is advanced in
Chap. ix. Book II. concerning the inconvenience of
great ftates; the matter in queftion there being the
authority of the government over its members, and
here of its influence over the fubjects. Its members,
fcattered about in different places, ferve as points
of fupport to enable it to act at a diftance on the people; but it hath no fuch props to affift its action
on its members themfelves. Thus in one cafe the
length of the lever is the caufe of its ftrength, and
in the other of its weaknefs.

habit

habited are the most proper places for tyrants; wild beasts reign only in desarts.

CHAP. IX.

Of the marks of a good Government.

WHEN it is asked, therefore, in general terms, what is the best form of government ? the question is as indeterminate as unanswerable : or rather it may be reasonably answered as many different ways as there are possible combinations of the absolute and relative circumstances of a people.

But if it be asked, by what signs it may be known whether any given people are well or ill governed ? This is quite another thing, and the question, as to the fact, is to be resolved.

This question, however, is never actually resolved, because every one is for doing it after his own manner. The subject cries up the public tranquillity, the citizen the liberty of individuals; the one prefers the security of property, the other that of his person ; the one maintains the best government to be the most severe, the other affirms that to be best which is most agreeable;

able; the latter is for punishing crimes, the
former for preventing them: the one thinks it
a fine thing to be dreaded by his neighbours;
the other thinks it better to be unknown to
them; the one is satisfied if money does but
circulate, the other requires the people should
have bread. Were they even agreed also on
these and other similar points, they would not
be much nearer the end of the dispute. Moral
quantities are deficient in point of precision;
so that, were men agreed on the sign, they
would still differ about its estimation.

For my part, I am astonished that a sign so
very simple should be mistaken, or that any
should be so disingenuous as not to acknowlege
it. What is the end of political society? doubtless the preservation and prosperity of its
members. And what is the most certain sign
or proof of these? Certainly it is their number
and population. Let us not look elsewhere,
then, for this disputed proof; since it is plain,
that government must be the best, under which
the citizens increase and multiply most, sup-
posing all other circumstances equal, and no
foreigners naturalized or colonies introduced,
to cause such increase: and that, on the

contrary

contrary, that government muſt be the worſt, under which, *cæteris paribus*, the number of people ſhould diminiſh. This being admitted, the deciſion of the queſtion becomes an affair of calculation *, and as ſuch I give it up to the arithmeticians.

CHAP.

* It is on the ſame principle that we ought to judge of the ſeveral periods of time that deſerve the preference, in being diſtinguiſhed for the proſperity of mankind. We have in general too much admired thoſe, in which literature and the fine arts have flouriſhed, without penetrating into the ſecret cauſe of their cultivation, or duly conſidering their fatal effects; *idque apud imperitos humanitas vocabatur, cum pars ſervitutis eſſet.* Shall we never be able to ſee through the maxims laid down in books, the intereſted motives of their authors?—No, let writers ſay what they will, whenever the inhabitants of a country decreaſe, it is not true that all things go well, whatever be its external proſperity and ſplendour: A poet poſſeſſed of an hundred thouſand livres a year, does not neceſſarily make the age he lives in the beſt of all others. We ſhould not ſo much regard the apparent repoſe of the world, and the tranquillity of its chiefs, as the well-being of whole nations, and particularly of the moſt populous ſtates. A ſtorm of hail may lay waſte ſome few provinces, but it ſeldom cauſes a famine. Temporary tumults and civil

CHAP. X.

Of the abuse of government, and its tendency to degenerate.

AS the particular will of the prince acts
constantly against the general will of the
people, the government necessarily makes a continual effort against the sovereignty. The greater
this effort is, the more is the constitution altered ; and as in this case there is no other distinct Will to keep that of the prince in equilibrio, it must sooner or later infallibly happen
that

civil wars may give much disturbance to rulers ; but
they do not constitute the real misfortunes of a people, who may even enjoy some respite, while they
are disputing who shall play the tyrant over them.
It is from their permanent situation that their real
prosperity or calamity must arise : when all submit
tamely to the yoke, then it is that all are perishing ;
then it is that their chiefs, destroying them at their ease,
ubi solitudinem faciunt pacem appellant. When the in-
trigues of the nobility agitated the kingdom of France,
and the coadjutor of Paris carried a poignard in his
pocket to parliament ; all this did not hinder the bulk
of the French nation from growing numerous and
en-

that the prince will opprefs the fovereign, and break the focial compact. This is an inherent and unavoidable defect, which from the very birth of the political body, inceffantly tends to its diffolution, even as old age and death tend to the diffolution of the natural body.

There are two general methods according to which a government degenerates; viz. when it contracts itfelf, or when the ftate is diffolved. The government contracts itfelf, when its members are reduced from a great number to a few; that is to fay, from a democracy to an ariftocracy, and from an ariftocracy to a royalty.

enjoying themfelves in happinefs and eafe. Ancient Greece flourifhed in the midft of the moft cruel wars: human blood was fpilt in torrents, and yet the country fwarmed with inhabitants. It appears, fays Machiavel, that, in the midft of murders, profcriptions and civil wars, our republic became only the more powerful, the virtue of the citizens, their manners, their independence had a greater effect to ftrengthen it, than all its diffentions had to weaken it. A little agitation gives vigour to the mind, and liberty, not peace, is the real fource of the profperity of our fpecies.

H   This

This is its natural tendency *. Should it make a retrogreffive change, by having the number of

* The flow formation and progrefs of the republic of Venice, prefent a notable example of this fucceffion; and it is very furprifing that in the fpace of 1200 years the Venetians fhould be got no farther than to the fecond term, which began in the year 1198. With regard to the ancient dukes, with which their conftitution is reproached, it is certain, whatever fome writers may fay, that they were not fovereigns.

The Roman republic will, doubtlefs, be made an objection, as having taken a contrary route, in its progrefs from monarchy to ariftocracy, and from ariftocracy to democracy. I am, however, far from thinking this was the real cafe.

The firft eftablifhment of Romulus was a mix$_t$ government, which degenerated prefently into defpotifm. From very particular caufes the ftate perifhed before its time, as a new born infant, before it attained the age of manhood. The expulfion of the Tarquins, was the true era of the rife of that republic; although it did not affume at firft a determinate form; becaufe the work was but half done, in not having abolifhed the order of patricians. For hence, an hereditary ariftocracy, the worft of all adminiftrations, of its members increased, it might be said to relax or dilate itself; but this inverse progress is impossible.

In fact, a government never changes its form, except its spring of action be too much worn to support its own. Now, if it relaxes still more, by being extended, its force becomes absolutely nothing,

strations, acting in opposition to the democracy, the form of government remained indeterminate; not being fixed, as Machiavel observes, till the establishment of the tribunes; when, and not before, it was a real government under the form of a true democracy. In fact, the people were then not only sovereign, but also magistrate and judge; the senate being a tribunal of an inferior order, formed to temper and collect the government; while even the consuls themselves although patricians, first magistrates, and as generals absolute in the field, yet at Rome they were only presidents of the assemblies of the people.

From this time it is evident the government followed its natural byas, and tended strongly toward aristocracy. The patrician order dying away of itself, the aristocracy subsisted no longer in the members of that body, as at Venice and Genoa, but in the body of the senate composed of Patricians and Plebeians, and even in the body of tribunes when they

H 2   began

nothing, and is ſtill leſs capable of ſupporting itſelf. It is neceſſary therefore to wind up and renew ſuch ſpring in proportion as it gives way; otherwiſe the ſtate it is intended to ſupport, muſt neceſſarily fall.

The diſſolution of the ſtate indeed may happen two ways. Firſt, when the prince does not govern according to law; but arrogates the ſovereign power to himſelf: in which caſe he effects a remarkable change, whereby not the government, but the ſtate itſelf is contracted. What I mean to ſay is, that the great ſtate is thence diſſolved, and that he forms another within it, compoſed only of the members of the government, who are only the maſters and tyrants over the reſt of the people. So

began to uſurp an active power. For words make no alteration in things. When the people have chiefs who govern in their ſtead, whatever denomination be given to thoſe chiefs, the government is always an ariſtocracy. From the abuſe of the ariſtocratical form, aroſe the civil wars and the triumvirate. Sylla, Julius Cæſar and Auguſtus indeed became real monarchs, and at length under the deſpotiſm of Tiberius the ſtate was finally diſſolved. The Roman hiſtory, therefore, doth not tend to diſprove my principle, but to confirm it.

that

that when the government ufurps the fovereignty, at that inftant the focial compact is broken,
and the individuals, who were citizens before,
are reftored to the rights of natural liberty,
and are compelled, not legally obliged, to
obedience.

It is the fame thing, when the members of
government affume feparately the power they
are entitled to exercife only collectively; which
is no lefs an infringement of the laws, and is
productive of ftill worfe confequences. For,
in this cafe, there may be faid to be as many
princes as magiftrates; while the ftate no lefs
divided than the government, is totally diffolved
or changes its form.

When the ftate is diffolved, the abufe of
government, of whatever nature it be, takes
the common name of anarchy. To diftinguifh
more nicely, *democracy* is faid to degenerate into
ochlocracy; *ariftocracy* into *oligarchy*; and I
may add *monarchy* into *tyranny*: but this laft
term is equivocal, and requires fome explanation. In the vulgar fenfe of the word, a tyrant
is a king who governs by force and without
regard to juftice or the laws. In the more precife and determinate fenfe, it means any indi-

H 3

vidual

vidual who affumes the royal authority, without having a right to it. In this latter fenfe the
Greeks underftood the word tyrant; and give
it indifcriminately both to good and bad princes
whofe authority was not legal *. Thus, *tyrant* and *ufurper* are two words perfectly fy-
nonimous.

To give different names, however, to different things, I call the ufurpation of regal authority, *tyranny*, and that of fovereign power
defpotifm. The tyrant is he, who takes
upon himfelf, contrary to law, to govern according to law; and the defpotic chief, one
who places himfelf above the laws themfelves.
Thus a tyrant cannot be defpotic, though a
defpotic prince muft always be a tyrant.

* *Omnes enim et habentur et dicuntur tyranni qui
poteftate utuntur perpetuâ, in eâ civitate quæ libertate
ufa eft.* CORN. NEPOS. IN MILTIADE. It is true
that Ariftotle makes a diftinction between the tyrant
and king, in that the one governs for his own good,
and the other for the good of his fubjects: but, befides that all the Greek writers ufe the word tyrant
in a different fenfe, as appears particularly by the
Hieron of Zenophon, it would follow from Ariftotle's
diftinction, that no king ever exifted on the face of
the earth.

CHAP.

CHAP. XI.

Of the diſſolution of the body politic.

SUCH is the natural and unavoidable tendency of even the beſt conſtituted governments. If Rome and Sparta periſhed, what
ſtate can hope to laſt for ever? In our endeavours to form a durable eſtabliſhment, we muſt
not think, therefore, to make it eternal. If we
would hope to ſucceed, we muſt not attempt
impoſſibilities, nor flatter ourſelves to give that
permanency to human inſtitutions, which is incompatible with their nature.

The body politic, as well as the phyſical,
begins to die at its birth, and bears in itſelf the
cauſes of its deſtruction. Both, however, may
poſſeſs a conſtitution more or leſs robuſt, and
adapted to different periods of duration. The
conſtitution of man is the work of nature; that
of the ſtate, is the work of art. It doth not
depend on men to prolong their lives, but it
depends on them to prolong that of the ſtate
as much as poſſible, by giving it a conſtitution
the beſt adapted to longevity. The moſt perfect conſtitution, it is true, will have an end;

H 4   but

but still so much later than others, if no unforeseen accident bring it to an untimely diffolution.

The principle of political life, lies in the
fovereign authority. The legiflative power is
the heart of the ftate; the executive power is
the brain, which puts every part in motion,
The brain may be rendered ufelefs by the palfy,
and yet the individual furvive. A man may become an infenfible driveller and yet live: but
as foon as the heart ceafes to beat, the animal
is dead.

The ftate doth not fubfift by virtue of the
laws, but by the legiflative power. The fla-
tutes of yefterday are not in themfelves neceffarily binding to day, but the tacit confirmation
of them is prefumed from the filence of the
legiflature; the fovereign being fuppofed inceffantly to confirm the laws not actually repealed. Whatever is once declared to be the
will of the fovereign, continues always fo, unlefs it be abrogated.

Wherefore, then, is there fo much refpect
paid to ancient laws? Even for this reafon. It
is rational to fuppofe, that nothing but the
ex-

excellence of the ancient laws, could preserve
them so long in being; for that, if the sovereign had not found them always salutary and
useful, they would have been repealed.

Hence we see that the laws, instead of losing
their force, acquire additional authority by
time, in every well formed state; the prepos-
session of their antiquity renders them every day
more venerable; whereas, in every country
where the laws grow obsolete and lose their
force as they grow old, this alone is a proof
that the legislative power itself is decayed, and
the state extinct.

CHAP. XII.

*By what means the sovereign authority is main-
tained.*

THE sovereign, having no other force
than the legislative power, acts only by
the laws; while the laws being only the authentic acts of the general will, the sovereign
cannot act unless the people are assembled. The
people assemble! you will say. What a chimera?—It is indeed chimerical at present;
though it was not reckoned so two thou-

H 5   sand

fand years ago. Are mankind changed in their nature fince that time?

The bounds of poffibility in moral affairs are lefs confined than we are apt to imagine: It is our foibles, our vices, our prejudices that con- tract them. Mean fouls give no credit to the fentiments of heroic minds; while flaves affect to turn the notion of liberty, into ridicule.

By what hath been done, however, we may judge of what may be done again. I fhall not fpeak of the petty republics of ancient Greece; but the Roman republic was, undoubtedly, a great ftate, and the city of Rome a great city. By the laft regifter of the citizens of Rome, their number amounted to four hundred thou- fand perfons capable of bearing arms; and the laft regifter of the Empire amounted to more than four millions of citizens, without reckon- ing fubjects, women, children or flaves.

How very difficult, you will fay, muft it have been, to affemble frequently the people of that capital and its environs? And yet hardly a week paffed in which the Roman people were not affembled, and on fome occafions feveral times a week.

I

a week. This numerous body indeed not only exercifed the functions of fovereignty, but alfo in fome cafes thofe of government. They fometimes deliberated on ftate affairs, and at others decided in judicial caufes; the whole people being publicly affembled almoft as frequently in the capacity of magiftrates as citizens.

By recurring to the primitive ftate of nations, we fhall find that moft of the ancient governments, even the monarchical, as that of the Macedon and others, had the like popular affemblies. Be this, however, as it may, the fact being once inconteftibly proved, obviates all difficulties; for, to deduce the poffibility of a thing from its having actually happened, will admit of no objection.

H 6   CHAP.

CHAP. XIII.

The subject continued.

IT is not enough, however, that the people once assembled should fix the constitution of the state, by giving their sanction to a certain code or system of laws : it is not enough that they should establish a perpetual government, or provide once for all by the election of magistrates. Besides the extraordinary assemblies, which unforeseen accidents may require, it is necessary they should have certain fixed and periodical meetings, which nothing might abolish or prorogue : so that the people should, on a certain day, be legally summoned by law, without any express statute being required for their formal convocation.

But, excepting these regular assemblies, rendered legal by the date, all others, unless convoked by the proper magistrate previously appointed to that end, agreeable to prescribed forms, should be held illegal, and all their determinations declared null and void; because the very manner of the people's assembling should be determined by law.

As

As to the frequency of legal affemblies, it depends on fo many different confiderations, that it is impoffible to lay down any precife rules on this head. It can only be faid in general that the more powerful the government, the more often ought the fovereignty to difplay itfelf.

All this, it may be faid, is very well for a fingle town or city; but what muft be done in a ftate comprehending feveral cities? Muft the fovereign authority be diftributed, or ought it to centre in one, to the total fubjection of the reft?

I anfwer, neither one nor the other. In the firft place, the fovereign authority is fimple and uniform, fo that it cannot be divided without deftroying it. In the next place, one city cannot be legally fubject to another, any more than one nation to another; becaufe the effence of the body-politic confifts in the union of obedience and liberty, and in the terms *fubject* and *fovereign* being thofe identical correlatives, the ideas of which are united in the fingle term *citizen*.

I anfwer

I anfwer farther, that it is fundamentally wrong, to unite feveral towns to form one city; and that fuch union being made, the natural inconveniences of it muft enfue. The abufes peculiar to great ftates muft not be made objections to the fyftem of one, who maintains the exclufive propriety of little ones. But how, it will be faid, can little ftates be made powerful enough to refift the great ?—Even as the cities of ancient Greece were able to refift the arms of a powerful monarch; and, as in more modern times, Switzerland and Holland, have refifted the power of the houfe of Auftria.

In cafes, alfo, where the ftate cannot be reduced within proper bounds, there remains one refource; and this is by not permitting the exiftence of a capital, but removing the feat of government from one town to another, and affembling the ftates of the country in each alternately.

People a country equally in every patt; diffufe the fame privileges and advantages throughout; and the ftate will become at once the ftrongeft and the beft governed. Remember that the walls of cities are founded on the ruins of the villages, and that the fplendid palaces

in

in town are raifed at the expence of miferable
cottages in the country.

CHAP. XIV.

Subject continued.

NO fooner are the people legally affembled,
in a fovereign body, than the jurifdiction
of government ceafes, the executive power of
the ftate is fufpended, and the perfon of the
meaneft citizen becomes as facred and inviolable
as the greateft magiftrate; becaufe when the
body reprefented appears, it is not requifite
that the reprefentatives of it fhould exift. Moft
of the tumults which happened in the *Comitia*
at Rome, were owing to the general ignorance
or neglect of this rule. On thofe occafions,
the confuls were only prefidents of the affembly
of the people, the tribunes merely orators *,
and the fenate abfolutely nothing.

Thefe intervals of fufpenfion, when the
prince acknowleges, or at leaft ought to ac-

---

* Nearly in the fenfe given to thofe who fpeak
on any queftion in the parliament of England. The
refemblance of their employments fet the confuls
and tribunes together by the ears; even when their
jurifdiction was fufpended.

knowlege

knowlege an actual fuperior, have been always
formidable, while fuch formidable affemblies,
the fecurity of the body politic and the reftraint
of government, have been held in honour by
the chiefs : fo that they never have been fparing
of pains, in raifing objections and difficulties,
or of making fair promifes in order to difguft
the citizens with fuch meetings. When the
latter, therefore, have been avaritious, mean,
or cowardly, preferring their cafe to liberty,
they have not been able to withftand long the repeated efforts of government : and thus it is
that, this encroaching power inceffantly aug-
menting, the fovereignty becomes totally extinct, and thus moft cities come to an untimely end.

Sometimes, however, there is introduced between fovereign authority and arbitrary government, a mean term of power, of which it
is neceffary to treat.

CHAP.

CHAP. XV.

Of deputies or representatives.

WHEN the service of the public ceases to be the principal concern of the citizens, and they had rather discharge it by their purses than their persons, the state is already far advanced toward ruin. When they should march out to fight, they pay troops to fight for them, and stay at home. When they should go to council, they send deputies, and stay at home. Thus, in consequence of their indolence and wealth, they in the end employ soldiers to enslave their country, and representatives to betray it.

It is the bustle of commerce and the arts; it is the sordid love of gain, of luxury and ease, that thus convert personal into pecuniary services. Men readily give up one part of their profit, to increase the rest unmolested. But supply an administration with money, and they will presently supply you with chains. The very term of *taxes* is slavish, and unknown in a free city. In a state truly free, the citizens discharge their duty to the public with their
own

own hands, and not by money. So far from
paying for being exempted from fuch duty,
they would pay to be permitted to difcharge it
themfelves. I am very far from adopting received opinions, and think the fervices exacted
by force a lefs infringement of liberty than
taxes.

The better the conftitution of a ftate, the
greater influence have public affairs over private,
in the minds of the citizens : They will have,
alfo, much fewer private affairs to concern
them; becaufe the fum total of their common
happinefs, furnifhing a more confiderable portion to each individual, there remains the lefs
for each to feek from his own private concerns.
In a city well governed, every one is ready to
fly to its public affemblies ; under a bad government they are carelefs about going thither at
all; becaufe no one interefts himfelf in what
is doing there ; it is known that the general
will does not influence them, and hence at
length domeftic concerns engage all their attention. Good laws tend to the making better,
while bad ones are introductory of Worfe. No
fooner doth a citizen fay, what are ftate-affairs
to me ? than the ftate may be given up for
loft.

It

It is this want of public fpirit, the influence of private intereft, the extent of ftates, conquefts and abufes in government, that have given rife to the method of affembling the people by deputies and reprefentatives. THe affembly of thefe reprefentatives is called in fome countries, the third eftate of the nation; fo that the particular interefts of the two orders are placed in the firft and fecond rank, and the public intereft only in the third.

The fovereignty, however, cannot be reprefented, and that for the fame reafon that it cannot be alienated. It confifts effentially of the general will, and the will cannot be reprefented : it is either identically the fame, or fome other ; there can be no mean term in the cafe. The deputies of the people, therefore, neither are nor can be their reprefentatives; they are only mere commiffioners, and can conclude definitively on nothing. Every law that is not confirmed by the people in perfon is null and void; it is not in fact a law. The Englifh imagine they are a free people; they are however miftaken : they are fuch only during the election of members of parliament. When thefe are chofen, they become flaves again; and indeed they make fo bad a ufe of the few

tran-

tranfitory moments of liberty, that they richly deferve to lofe it.

The notion of reprefentatives is modern; defcending to us from the feudal fyftem, that moft iniquitous and abfurd form of government, by which human nature was fo fhamefully degraded. In the ancient republics, and even monarchies, the people had no reprefentatives; they were ftrangers to the term. It is even very fingular that, at Rome, where the Tribunes were fo much revered, it was never imagined they could ufurp the functions of the people; and as ftrange that they never once attempted it. One may judge, however, of the embarraffment fometimes caufed by the multitude, by what happened in the time of the Gracchi, when part of the citizens gave their votes from their houfe-tops.

Where men value their liberty and privileges above every thing, inconveniences and difficulties are nothing. Among this wife people things were held in a proper eftimation; they permitted the Lictors to do what they would not fuffer the Tribunes to attempt; they were not

afraid

afraid the Lictors would ever think of repre-
fenting them.

To explain, neverthelefs, in what manner
thefe Tribunes did fometimes reprefent them,
it will be fufficient to conceive how government reprefents the fovereign. The law being
only a declaration of the general will, it is clear
that the people cannot be reprefented in the legiflative power ; but they may, and ought to be, in
the executive ; which is only the application of
power to law. And this makes it evident that,
if we examine things to the bottom, we fhall
find very few nations that have any laws. But,
be this as it may, it is certain that the Tribunes, having no part of the executive power,
could not reprefent the Roman people, by virtue of their office, but only in ufurping thofe
of the fenate.

Among the Greeks, whatever the people had
to do, they did it in perfon ; they were perpetually affembled in public. They inhabited
a mild climate, were free from avarice, their
flaves managed their domeftic bufinefs, and
their great concern was liberty. As you do not
poffefs the fame advantages, how can you expect

pect to preserve the same privileges ? Your climate being more severe, creates more wants * ;
for six months in the year your public squares
are too wet or cold to be frequented; your
hoarse tongues cannot make themselves heard
in the open air; you apply yourselves more to
gain than to liberty, and are less afraid of slavery
than poverty.

On this occasion, it will probably be asked
me, if liberty cannot support itself without the
assistance of slavery ? Perhaps not.   At least
the two extremes approach very near.   Whatever does not exist in nature, must have its
conveniences, and civil society still more than
any thing else.   There are some circumstances
so critically unhappy that men cannot preserve
their own liberty but at the expence of the liberty of others; and in which a citizen cannot
be perfectly free without aggravating the subjection of his slaves.   Such was the situation
of Sparta.   As for you, ye moderns, you have
no slaves, but are slaves yourselves, and purchase

* To adopt in cold countries the luxury and ef-
feminacy of the East, is to appear desirous of slavery, without having the same excuse for submitting
to it.

their

their liberty by your own. You may if you pleafe boaft of this preference; for my part, I find more meannefs in it than humanity.

I do not intend, however, by this to inculcate that we fhould have flaves, or that it is equitable to reduce men to a ftate of flavery; having already proved the contrary. I am here only giving the reafons why certain modern nations who imagine themfelves free, employ reprefentatives, and why the ancients did not. But let this be as it will, I affirm that when once a people make choice of reprefentatives, they are no longer free.

Every thing duly confidered, I do not fee a poffibility of the fovereign maintaining its rights, and the exercife of its prerogatives, for the future among us, unlefs the ftate be indeed very fmall. But if it be fo very fmall, will it not be liable to lofe its independency? No. I will make it hereafter appear in what manner the exterior power of a great people may be united with the policy and good order of a little one.

CHA

CHAP. XVI.

That the institution of government is not a compact.

THE legislative power being once well
established, we proceed to settle the executive power in the same manner : for the
latter which operates only by particular acts,
being essentially different from the other, is naturally divided from it. If it were possible
for the sovereign, considered as such, to possess
the executive power, the matter of right and
fact would be so confounded, that we should
no longer be able to distinguish what is law and
what is not ; the body politic also being thus
unnaturally situated, would soon become a prey
to that violence, which it was originally instituted to correct.

The citizens being, by virtue of the social
compact, all equal, that which all may perform,
all may prescribe, whereas none can have a
right to require another to do what he does not
himself.   Now it is properly this right, indispen-
sibly necessary to animate and put the body politic in motion, with which the sovereign in-
vests

vefts the prince in the inftitution of government.

It has been pretended by fome that the act
forming this inftitution, was a contract between
the people and the chiefs of which they
made choice: a contract in which the two
parties ftipulated the conditions on which the
one obliged themfelves to command, and the
other to obey. I am perfuaded every one will
agree with me that this was a very ftrange mode
of contract. But let us fee whether this opinion is in itfelf well founded.

In the firft place the fupreme authority can
no more modify or alter its form than it can
alienate itfelf; to limit or reftrain, would be
to deftroy it. It is abfurd and contradictory
to fay the fovereign made choice of a fuperior:
to oblige itfelf to obey a mafter, is to diffolve
its own conftitution, and reftore its members
to their natural liberty.

Again, it is plain that fuch a fuppofed contract between the people in general and certain
particular perfons would be a particular act;
whence it follows that it would not be a law

nor

nor an act of sovereignty, and of consequence would be illegal.

It is farther evident, that the contracting parties would remain, respecting each other, simply under the laws of nature, without any security for the performance of their reciprocal engagements, a circumstance totally repugnant to a state of civil society. The party only who might have the power, could enforce the execution of the terms; so that we might as well give the name of a contract, to the act of a man who should say to another, " I give you my whole property, on condition that you will restore me just as much of it as you please."

There is but one compact in a state, and that is the act of association, which alone is exclusive of every other; as it is impossible to imagine any subsequent public contract which would not be a violation of the original.

CHAP.

CHAP. XVII.

Of the inftitution of government.

WHAT notion, then, are we to form of the act, by which government is inftituted ? In anfwer to this queftion, I fhall firft remark that this act is complicated, or compofed of two others, viz the eftablifhment of the law and the execution of it.

By the firft, the fovereign enacts that a government fhall be eftablifhed in fuch or fuch a form ; and it is clear, this being a general act, that it is a law.

By the fecond, the people name the chiefs who are to be charged with the adminiftration of the government fo eftablifhed. Now this nomination, being a particular act, is not a fecond law, but only a confequence of the firft, and in reality an act of government.

The difficulty lies in being able to comprehend how an act of government can take place before the government exifted, and how the

people,

people, who muſt be always either ſovereign or
ſubjeɛts, become prince or magiſtrate, in certain circumſtances.

We have here made a diſcovery of one of
theſe aſtoniſhing properties of the body politic,
by which it reconciles operations apparently
contradiɛtory to each other ; this aɛt being ef-
feɛted by a ſudden converſion of the ſovereignty
into a democracy : ſo that, without any ſenſible
change, and only by means of a new relation of
all to all, the citizens, becoming magiſtrates,
paſs from general aɛts to particular ones, and
from enaɛting laws to the execution of them.

This change of relation is not a matter of
mere ſpeculation, unexemplified in praɛtice :
it takes place very frequently in the parliament
of England, where among the commons, the
whole houſe is formed on certain occaſions, into
a committee, for the better enquiry into, and
diſcuſſion of the matter in hand ; the members
become mere commiſſioners of the ſovereign
court they conſtituted but a moment before.
Agreeable to which, the enquiry being ended,
they make a report to themſelves, as the houſe
of Commons, of their proceedings as a grand
                                            com-

committee, and deliberate anew under the former title on what they had already determined under the latter.

Such, indeed, is the peculiar advantage of a democratical government, that it is established in fact by the simple act of the general will. After which, this provisional government continues, if such be the intended form; or establishes, in the name of the sovereign, the form of government adopted by law; and thus every thing proceeds according to order. It is impossible to institute a government in any other legal manner, without renouncing the principles before established.

CHAP. XVIII.

Of the means of preventing the usurpations of government.

FROM the foregoing illustrations results the confirmation of what is asserted in the XVIth chapter, viz. that the act which institutes government is not a contract but a law; that the depositories of the executive power are

I 3   not

not the mafters, but the fervants of the people;
that the people may appoint or remove them
at pleafure; that they have no pretence to a contract with the people, but are bound to obey
them; and that in accepting the offices the
ftate impofes on them, they only difcharge
their duty as citizens, without having any fort
of right to difpute the conditions.

When it fo happens, therefore, that the
people eftablifh an hereditary government,
whether monarchical, and confined to one
particular family, or ariftocratical, and divided
among a certain order of citizens, they do not
enter thereby into any formal engagement; they
only give the adminiftration a provifional form,
which remains legal till they think proper to
change it.

It is certain that fuch changes are always
dangerous, and that a government once eftablifhed fhould not be meddled with, unlefs it
be found incompatible with the public good;
but this circumfpection is a maxim of policy,
and not a matter of right. The ftate, however, is no more bound to refign the civil authority

thority into the hands of its magiftrates or chiefs, than the military authority into thofe of its generals.

It is certain, alfo, that great care fhould be taken to obferve all thofe formalities, which, in fuch a cafe, are requifite to diftinguifh a regular and legal act from a feditious commotion; to diftinguifh between the general will of a whole people and the clamours of a faction. In which latter cafe, a people are particularly obliged to give the beft founded remonftrances no farther countenance, than in the utmoft ftrictnefs of juftice they may deferve. Of this obligation, however, the prince may take great advantages, in order to preferve his power in fpite of the people, without running the rifk of being charged with ufurping it. For in appearing only to make ufe of his prerogatives, he may extend them, and under the pretence of maintaining the public peace, may prevent thofe affemblies which might otherwife be calculated to re-eftablifh the good order of government: fo that he might profit by that filence which he keeps from being broken, and by thofe ir-

regularities which he himfelf might caufe to
be committed ; pleading in his favour the tacit approbation of thofe whofe fears keep them
filent ; and punifhing thofe who are bold
enough to fpeak. It was thus the *decemviri,*
at firft elected for one year only, and afterwards continued for another, attempted to perpetuate the duration of their power, by preventing the *Comitia* from affembling as ufual ;
and it is by fuch eafy means that all the governments in the world, when once invefted
with power, ufurp fooner or later the fovereign
authority.

Thofe periodical affemblies, of which I
have fpoken above, are very proper to prevent,
or protract, this misfortune, particularly when
they require no formal convocation ; for then
the prince cannot prevent them without declaring himfelf openly a violator of the laws,
and an enemy to the ftate.

The opening of thefe affemblies, which have
no other object than the prefervation of the
focial contract, ought always to be made. by
two

two propofitions, which can never be fup-preffed, and fhould pafs feparately by vote.

FIRST; Whether it be the determination of the fovereign to preferve the prefent form of government.

SECOND; Whether it be the determination of the people to continue the adminiftration in the hands of thofe, who are at prefent charged with it.

It is to be obferved, that I here take for granted, what I conceive has already been demonftrated, viz. that there is no fundamental law in any ftate, which fuch ftate cannot repeal, not excepting even the focial compact: for, fhould all the citizens affemble with one accord to break this compact, it would un-doubtedly be very legally diffolved. Grotius even thinks that an individual may renounce the ftate of which he is a member, and re-fume his natural independence and property by leaving the country *. Now it would be very

---

* With this exception, however, that he does not fly, to elude his duty, and avoid fervirg his coun-

try

very abſurd to ſuppoſe that the whole body of citizens united, could not do that in con-cert, which any one of them might do ſepa-rately.

try on any emergency, when his ſervice is required. In this caſe his flight would be criminal and highly deſerving of puniſhment. It would not be a retreat but deſertion.

The END of the THIRD BOOK.

BOOK

BOOK IV.

CHAP. I.

That the general will cannot be annihilated.

SO long as a number of individuals remain perfectly united and confider themfelves as one body, they can have but one will; which relates to their common prefervation and welfare. All the refources of the ftate, are then fimple and vigorous, its political maxims clear and obvious; it comprehends no intricate and oppofite interefts; but that of the public is demonftrably evident to all, and requires only the gift of common fenfe to underftand it. Peace, concord, and equality are enemies to political refinements. When men are honeft, and fimple, their very fimplicity prevents their deception; they are not to be impofed on by fophiftry, but are too artlefs even to be duped. When it is known, that, among the happieft people in the world, a number of peafants meet together under the fhade of an oak, and regulate the affairs of ftate, with the moft prudential œconomy, is it poffible to forbear de-

I 6   *fpifing*

spifing the refinements of other nations, who employ fo much artifice and myftery to render themfelves fplendidly miferable ?

A ftate thus fimply governed hath need of but few laws, while in proportion as it becomes neceffary to promulgate new ones, that neceffity is univerfally apparent. The firft perfon who propofes them, takes on himfelf to fpeak only what every one hath already thought; and neither eloquence nor intrigue is requifite to make that pafs into a law, which every one had already refolved to do, as foon as he fhould be affured others would do the fame.

That which deceives our reafoners on this fubject, is, that, feeing none but fuch ftates as were badly conftituted at their beginning, they are ftruck with the impoffibility of maintaining fuch a police in them. They fmile to think of the abfurdities, into which a defigning knave or infinuating orator might lead the people of Paris and London. They are not apprized that a Cromwell, and a Beaufort, would have been treated as incendiaries at Berne and Geneva, and have underwent the difcipline due to their demerit.

But

But when the bonds of fociety begin to relax, and the ftate to grow weak; when the private interefts of individuals begin to appear, and that of parties to influence the ftate, the ob- jeéts of public good meet with oppofition; un- animity no longer prefides in the affemblies of the people; the general will is no longer the will of all; contradiétions and debates arife, and the moft falutary counfel is not adopted without difpute.

Again, when the ftate is bordering on ruin, and exifts only in empty form, when the focial tie no longer conneéts the hearts of the people, when the bafeft motives of intereft impudently affume the facred name of the public good; then is the general will altogether filent; indi- viduals, aétuated by private motives, cherifh no more the fentiments of citizens, than if the ftate had never exifted, while the mock legif- lature pafs, under the name of laws, thofe ini- quitous decrees which have no other end than private intereft.

Doth it follow from hence, however, that the general will is annihilated or corrupted? No. This remains ever conftant, invariable, and

and pure; though it is subjected to that of party. There is not an individual who doth not see, while he detaches his own interest from that of the public, that he cannot separate himself from it entirely: but his share in the common evil seems nothing in comparison to the good which he proposes to secure exclusively to himself. Setting this motive aside, he is as ready to concur in measures for the good of the public, and that even for his own sake as any one. Nay, even in selling his vote, he doth not lose all sense of the general will; he only eludes it. The fault he is guilty of, lies in changing the state of the question, and making an answer to what is not asked him; so that, instead of admitting by his vote, *that it is to the interest of the state*, he says, *it is to the interest of such an individual or such a party, that this or that law should pass*. Thus the order which should prevail in the public assemblies of the state, should not be calculated so much to preserve the general will inviolate, as to cause it to be always interrogated, and to make it answer.

I might here make a variety of reflections on the simple right of voting in every act of the sovereignty; a right which the citizens cannot be deprived of: as also on the rights of think-

thinking, propofing and debating on public matters; privileges which government is ever folicitous enough to confine to its own members. This fubject, however, is of importance enough to deferve a whole treatife of itfelf; and it is impoffible for me to fay every thing in the prefent.

CHAP. II.

On Votes.

IT is evident, from what hath been faid in the preceding chapter, that the manner in which public affairs are carried on, may afford a fure indication of the actual ftate of manners, and the health of the body politic. The more concord there is in public affemblies, that is to fay, the nearer the members approach to unanimity in giving their votes, the more prevalent is the general will among them: but long debates, diffentions and commotions, evince the afcendency of particular interefts and the decline of the ftate.

This appears lefs evident, indeed, when two or more orders of men, enter into the conftitution; as at Rome, where the quarrels of the

Pa-

Patricians and Plebeians occafioned frequent di-
fturbances in the *Comitia*, even in the moft flou-
rifhing times of the republic. This exception
however, is more apparent than real : as in that
cafe there exifts, by a defect inherent in the
body politic, two ftates in one; and that which
is not true of both together, may neverthelefs
be true of each apart. It is alfo true in fact
that, even during the moft turbulent times of
the republic, the decrees of the Plebeians, when
he Senate did not intermeddle, were paffed
with great tranquillity agreeable to the plurality of voices. The citizens having but one
common intereft, the people could have but one
will.

Unanimity returns again at the oppofite ex-
tremity of the circle ; and this is where the citizens, reduced to flavery, have neither liberty
nor will. In fuch a fituation, fear and flattery
pervert their votes into acclamations; they no
longer deliberate among themfelves ; but either
adore or curfe their tyrants. Such were the
debafed principles of the Senate under the Roman emperors. Under thefe circumftances alfo,
the fentiments of the public were frequently
expreffed, with the moft ridiculous precau-
tion ; Tacitus obferving that, under Otho, the
Se-

Senators, while they loaded Vitellius with exe-
crations, they affected at the same time to
make a confused and clamorous noise, in order
to prevent his knowing, should he become
their master, what any individual had said.

From these considerations may be deduced
the maxims, on which the manner of counting
votes, and comparing different suffrages, should
be regulated, according as the general will is more
or less easy to be discovered, and the state more
or less advanced towards its decline. There is
but one law, which in its own nature, requires
unanimous consent: and this is the social compact. For civil association is the most voluntary act in the world : every man being born
free, and master of himself, no one can lay him
under restraint, on any pretence whatever,
without his own consent. To affirm that the
son of a slave is born a slave, is to affirm he is
not born a man.

If there be any persons, however, who op-
pose this contract itself, their opposition does
not invalidate that contract; it only hinders
their being comprehended therein ; and they remain aliens in the midst of citizens. When
a state

a ſtate is formed, a conſent to its inſtitution is
inferred by the reſidence of the party: to ſubmit to reſidence in any country is to ſubmit to its
ſovereignty *.

If we except this primitive contract, the determination of the majority is always obligatory on the reſt: this is a neceſſary conſequence
of the contract itſelf. But it may be aſked,
how can a man be free, and yet be obliged to
conform to the will of others. How can the
members of an oppoſition be called free-men,
who are compelled to ſubmit to laws which
they have not conſented to? I anſwer that this
queſtion is not properly ſtated. The citizen
conſents to all laws paſſed by a majority, though
ſome of them in particular may have paſſed contrary to his inclination; nay he conſents to thoſe
by which he is puniſhable for the breach of

* This muſt always be underſtood, however, of a
free ſtate, from which people have the liberty to de-
part with their effects at pleaſure. For in others the
conſideration of their family, their property, the
want of an aſylum, neceſſity or violence, may de-
tain an inhabitant in a country contrary to his will;
in which caſe, his ſimple reſidence neither implies
his conſent to the contract, nor his violation of it.

any

any one. The conftant will of all the members of a ftate, is the general will; and it is
this alone that makes them either citizens or
freemen *. When a law is propofed in the
affembly of the people, they are not precifely
demanded, whether they feverally approve or
reject the propofition; but whether it be conformable or not to the general will, which is
theirs as a collective body; each perfon, therefore, in giving his vote declares his opinion on
this head, and, on counting the votes, the declaration of the general will, is inferred from
the majority. When a law thus paffes contrary
to my opinion, it proves nothing more than
that I was miftaken, and that I concluded the
general will to be what it really was not. So
that, if my particular advice had been followed, it would have been contrary to my will,

* At Genoa we fee the word *Libertas* infcribed
on the chains of the galley flaves, and on the doors
of the prifoners: the application of which device is
beautiful and juft; as it is in fact only the criminals
of all ftates that infringe the liberty of the citizen.
A country, whofe malefactors fhould be all actually
chained to the oar, would be a country of the moft
perfect liberty.

which

which as a citizen is the fame as the general, and in that cafe I fhould not have been free.

This argument fuppofes, indeed, that all the characteriftics of the general will, are contained in the plurality of votes: and when this ceafes to be the cafe, take what courfe you will, there is an end of liberty.

In having fhewn how the will of particulars and parties is fubftituted for the general, in public deliberations, I have already fufficiently pointed out the practicable means of preventing fuch abufes ; of this, however, I fhall fpeak further hereafter. With regard to the proportional number of votes that indicate this general will, I have alfo laid down the principles on which it may be determined. The difference of a fingle voice is enough to break the unanimity ; but between unanimity and an equality there is a variety of proportions ; to each of which the number in queftion may be applied, according to the circumftances of the body politic.

There are two general maxims, which may ferve to regulate thefe proportions: the one is, that the more grave and important the deliberations,

the

the nearer ought the determination to approach
to unanimity: the other is, that the more expedition the affair requires, the lefs fhould unanimity be infifted on. In deliberations where
the matter fhould be immediately determined,
the majority of a fingle vote fhould be fufficient.
The firft of thefe maxims feems moft applicable
to permanent laws, and the fecond to matters
of bufinefs. But be this as it may, it is from
their judicious combination, that the beft proportions muft be deduced, concerning that plurality in whofe votes fhould be fuppofed to confift the general will.

C H A P. III.

Of Elections.

WITH regard to the election of a prince
or of magiftrates; which, as I before
obferved is a complicated act; there are two
methods of proceeding; viz. by choice and by
lot. They have each been made ufe of in different republics; and we fee in our own times,
a very intricate mixture of both in the election
of the doge of Venice.

The

The preference by lot, fays Montefquieu, *is of the nature of a democracy.* This I admit, but not for the reafons given. *The choice by lot,* fays he, *is a method which offends no-body ; by permitting each citizen to entertain the reafonable hope of being preferred to the fervice of his country.*

This, however, is not the true reafon. If we reflect that the election of chiefs is a function of government and not of the fovereignty, we fhall fee the reafon why this method is of the nature of a democracy, in which the adminiſtration is fo much the better, as its acts are fewer.

In every real democracy the office of magiftrate is not advantageous but expenfive and burthenfome, fo that it were unjuft to impofe it on one perfon rather than another. The law, therefore, impofes that charge on him, to whofe lot it falls. For in this cafe, all ftanding an equal chance, the choice doth not depend on human will, nor can any particular application change the univerfality of the law.

In an ariftocracy the prince makes choice of the prince ; and, the government providing for it-

itſelf, here it is that votes are properly applicable. The apparent exception, in the election of the doge of Venice, confirms this diſtinction, inſtead of deſtroying it : ſuch a mixt form as is uſed by the Venetians is adapted to a mixt government. For it is a miſtake to ſuppoſe the government of Venice a true ariſtocracy. If the lower order of people, indeed, have no ſhare in the government, the nobility ſtand in their place, and become the people in reſpect to the adminiſtration. What a number is there of the inferior order of nobles, who ſtand no chance of ever getting into the magiſtracy, and reap no other advantage from their rank than the empty title of Excellency, and the privilege of ſitting in the great Council. This great council being as numerous as our general council at Geneva, its illuſtrious members have no greater privileges therefore than our ordinary citizens. It is certain, that ſetting aſide the extreme diſparity of the two republics, the burghers of Geneva repreſent exactly the Patricians of Venice; our natives and ſojourners repreſent the citizens and people, and our peaſants the inhabitants of the *terra firma* belonging to that ſtate. In a word, conſider their Venetian republic in what light you will,

will, abſtracted from its grandeur, its government, is no more ariſtocratical than that of
Geneva. All the difference is that we have no
occaſion for this kind of election.

The choice by lot, is attended with very little
inconvenience in a real democracy, when all men
being nearly on an equality, as well with regard
to manners and abilities, as to ſentiments
and fortune, the matter of choice is indifferent.
But I have already obſerved a true democracy is
only imaginary.

. When the election is of a mixt form, viz.
by vote and by lot, the firſt ought to provide
for thoſe officers which require proper talents,
as in military affairs ; the other being beſt adapted to thoſe which require only common ſenſe,
honeſty and integrity; ſuch as the offices of
judicature; becauſe in a well-formed ſtate, thoſe
qualities are poſſeſſed by all the citizens in
common.

No election either by vote or lot, hath place
under a monarchical government ; the monarch
himſelf being the only rightful prince and legal
magiſtrate, the choice of his ſubſtitute is veſted
in

in him alone. When the Abbé de St. Pierre, therefore, propofed to increafe the number of the king's councils in France, and to elect their members by ballot, he was not aware that he propofed to change the form of the French government.

It remains to fpeak of the manner of giving and collecting votes in popular affemblies; but, perhaps, an hiftorical fketch of the Roman police relating to this point, will explain it better than all the maxims I fhould endeavour to eftablifh. It is worth the pains of a judicious reader, to attend a little particularly to the manner, in which they treated affairs, both general and particular, in a council of two hundred thoufand perfons.

K   C H A P.

CHAP. IV.

Of the Roman Comitia.

WE have no authentic monuments of the earliest ages of Rome; there is even great reason to believe that most of the stories told us of them are fabulous *; and indeed, the most interesting and instructive part of the annals of nations in general, which is that of their establishment, is the most imperfect. Experience daily teaches us to what causes are owing the revolutions of kingdoms and empires; but as we see no instances of the original formation of states, we can only proceed on conjectures in treating this subject.

The customs we find actually established, however, sufficiently attest, there must have been an origin of those customs. Those traditions,

* The name of *Rome*, which it is pretended was taken from *Romulus*, is Greek, and signifies *force*; the name of Numa is Greek also, and signifies *law*. What probability is there that the two first kings of this city should have been called by names so expressive of their future actions?

also,

alſo, relating to ſuch origin, which appear the
moſt rational, and of the beſt authority, ought
to paſs for the moſt certain. Theſe are the
maxims I have adopted in tracing the manner
in which the moſt powerful and free people in
the univerſe, exerciſed the ſovereign authority.

After the foundation of Rome, the riſing republic, that is to ſay, the army of the founder,
compoſed of Albans, Sabines and foreigners,
was divided into three claſſes; which, from that
diviſion, took the name of tribes. Each of
theſe tribes was ſubdivided into ten *Curiæ*, and
each *Curia* into *decuriæ*, at the head of which
were placed chiefs reſpectively denominated *cu-
rionus* and *decuriones.*

Beſide this, there were ſelected from each
tribe a body of an hundred cavaliers or knights,
called *centurions*; by which it is evident that
theſe diviſions, not being eſſential to the good
order of a city, were at firſt only military:
But it ſeems as if the preſaging inſtinct of future
greatneſs, induced the little town of Rome to
adopt at firſt a ſyſtem of police proper for the
metropolis of the world.

K 2   From

From this primitive divifion, however, there fpeedily refulted an inconvenience. This was that the tribe of Albans, and that of the Sabines always remaining the fame, while that of the ftrangers was perpetually encreafing by the concourfe of foreigners, the latter foon furpaffed the number of the two former. The remedy which Servius applied to correct this dangerous abufe was to change the divifion; and to fubftitute, in the room of diftinction of race, which he abolifhed, another taken from the parts of the town occupied by each tribe. Inftead of three tribes, he conftituted four; each of which occupied one of the hills of Rome, and bore its name. Thus by removing this inequality for the prefent, he prevented it alfo for the future; and in order that fuch divifion fhould not only be local but perfonal, he prohibited the inhabitants of one quarter of the city, from removing to the other, and thereby prevented the mixture of families.

He doubled alfo the three ancient centuries of cavalry, and made an addition of twelve others, but always under their old denomination; a fimple and judicious method, by which he compleatly diftinguifhed the body of knights
from

from that of the people, without exciting the murmurs of the latter.

Again, to thefe four city tribes, Servius added fifteen others, called ruftic tribes, becaufe they were formed of the inhabitants of the country, divided into as many cantons. In the fequel were made an equal number of new divifions, and the Roman people found themfelves divided into thirty-five tribes ; the number at which their divifions remained fixed, till the final diffolution of the republic.

From the diftinction between the tribes of city and country, refulted an effect worthy of obfervation ; becaufe we have no other example of it, and becaufe Rome was at once indebted to it for the prefervation of its manners and the increafe of its empire. It might be conceived the city tribes would foon arrogate to themfelves, the power and honours of the ftate, and treat the ruftics with contempt. The effect, neverthelefs, was directly contrary. The tafte of the ancient Romans for a country life is well known. They derived this tafte from the wife inftitutor, who joined to liberty the labours of the peafant and the foldier, and configned, as

K 3

it

it were, to the city, the cultivation of the arts, trade, intrigue, fortune and flavery.

Thus the moſt illuſtrious perſonages of Rome, living in the country, and employing themſelves in the buſineſs of agriculture, it was among theſe only the Romans looked for the defenders of their republic. This ſtation, being that of the moſt worthy patricians, was held in univerſal eſteem : the ſimple and laborious life of the villager was preferred to the mean and lazy life of the citizen; and a perſon who, having been a labourer in the country, became a reſpectable houſe-keeper in town, was yet held in contempt.   It is with reaſon, ſays Varro, that our magnanimous anceſtors eſtabliſhed in the country the nurſery for thoſe robuſt and brave men, who defended them in time of war and cheriſhed them in peace.   Again, Pliny ſays in expreſs terms, the country tribes were honoured becauſe of the perſons of which they were compoſed; whereas ſuch of their individuals as were to be treated with ignominy, were removed into the tribes of the city.   When the Sabine, Appius Claudius, came to ſettle in Rome, he was loaded with honours, and regiſtered in one of the ruſtic tribes, which afterwards took

the

the name of his family. Laftly, the freed-men were all entered in the city tribes, never in the rural; nor is there one fingle inftance, during the exiftence of the republic, of any one of thefe freedmen being preferred to the magiftracy, although become a citizen.

This was an excellent maxim, but was carried fo far, that it effected an alteration, and undoubtedly an abufe in the police of the ftate.

In the firft place, the Cenfors, after having long arrogated the right of arbitrarily removing the citizens from one tribe to another, permitted the greater part to regifter themfelves in whatever tribe they pleafed; a permiffion that could furely anfwer no good end, and yet it deprived thefe officers of one of their fevereft methods of cenfure. Befides, as the great and powerful thus got themfelves regiftered in the rural tribes; and the freedmen, with the populace, only filled up thofe of the city; the tribes in general had no longer a local diftinction: but were fo ftrangely mixed and jumbled together, that their refpective members could be known only by appealing to the regifters, fo that the idea attached to the word tribe,

was

was changed from real to perſonal, or rather became altogether chimerical.

It happened alſo that the tribes of the city, being nearer at hand, had generally the greateſt influence in the *Comitia*, and made a property of the ſtate, by ſelling their votes to thoſe who were baſe enough to purchaſe them.

With regard to the *Curiæ*, ten having been inſtituted in each tribe, the whole Roman people, included within the walls, made up thirty *Curiæ*, each of which had their peculiar temples, their gods, officers and feaſts called *Cimpitalia*, reſembling the *paganalia*, afterwards inſtituted among the ruſtic tribes.

At the new diviſion made by Servius, the number thirty not being equally diviſible among the four tribes, he forbore to meddle with this mode of diſtribution ; and the Curiæ, thus independent of the tribes, formed another diviſion of the inhabitants. No notice, however, was taken of the Curiæ, either among the ruſtic tribes, or the people compoſing them ; becauſe the tribes becoming a mere civil eſtabliſhment, and another method having been introduced for

raiſing

raifing the troops, the military diftinctions of Romulus were dropt as fuperfluous. Thus, though every citizen was regiftered in fome tribe, yet many of them were not included in any *curia*. Servius made ftill a third divifion, which had no relation to the two former, and became in its confequences the moft important of all. He divided the whole Roman people into fix claffes, which he diftinguifhed, neither by perfons nor place, but by property. Of thefe the higher claffes were filled by the rich, the lower by the poor, and the middle claffes by thofe of middling fortunes. Thefe fix claffes were fubdivided into one hundred ninety-three other bodies called centuries; and thefe were again fo diftributed that the firft clafs alone comprehended more than half the number of centuries, and the laft clafs only one fingle century. In this method the clafs that contained the feweft perfons, had the greater number of centuries; and the laft clafs was in number only a fubdivifion, although it contained more than half the inhabitants of Rome.

In order that the people fhould penetrate lefs into the defign of this latter form of diftribution, Servius affected to give it the air of a mi-

litary

litary one. In the fecond clafs he incorporated two centuries of armourers, and annexed two inftruments of war to the fourth. In each clafs, except the laft, he diftinguifhed alfo between the young and the old, that is to fay, thofe who were obliged to bear arms, from thofe who were exempted from it on account of their age; a diftinction which gave more frequent rife to the repetition of the *cenfus* or enumeration of them, than even the fhifting of property: laftly, he required their affembly to be made on the *Campus Martius,* where all thofe who were of age for the fervice were to appear under arms.

The reafon, why he did not purfue the fame diftinction of age in the laft clafs, was, that the populace, of which it was compofed, were not permitted to have the honour of bearing arms in the fervice of their country. It was neceffary to be houfe-keepers, in order to attain the privilege of defending themfelves. There is not one private centinel perhaps, of all thofe innumerable troops, that make fo brilliant a figure in the armies of modern princes, who would not, for want of property, have been driven out with difdain from a Roman Cohort, when foldiers were the defenders of liberty.

In

In the laſt claſs, however, there was a diſtinction made between what they called *proletarii* and
thoſe denominated *capite cenſi*. The former,
not quite reduced to nothing, ſupplied the ſtate
at leaſt with citizens, and ſometimes on preſſing
occaſions with ſoldiers. As to thoſe, who were
totally deſtitute of ſubſtance, and could be
numbered only by capitation, they were diſre-
garded as nothing; Marius being the firſt who
deigned to enroll them.

Without taking upon me here to decide, whether this third ſpecies of diviſion be in itſelf
good or ill; I may venture ſafely to affirm, that
nothing leſs than that ſimplicity of manners,
which prevailed among the ancient Romans,
their diſintereſtedneſs, their taſte for agriculture, their contempt for trade and the thirſt of
gain, could have rendered it practicable. Where
is the nation among the moderns, in which voracious avarice, a turbulence of diſpoſition, a
ſpirit of artifice, and the continual fluctuation
of property, would permit ſuch an eſtabliſhment to continue for twenty years without over-
turning the ſtate? Nay it muſt be well obſerved
that the purity of the Roman manners, and the
force of a cenſure more efficacious than the in-

K 6   ſtitution

ftitution itfelf, ferved to correct the defects of
it at Rome, where a rich man was often removed from his own clafs and ranked among the
poor, for making an improper parade of his
wealth.

It is eafy to comprehend from this, why mention is hardly ever made of more than five claffes,
though there were in reality fix.   The fixth,
furnifhing neither the army with foldiers, nor
the *Campus Martius* * with voters, and being
of hardly any ufe in the republic, was hardly
ever accounted any thing.

Such were the different divifions of the Roman people.   We will now examine into the defects, of which they were productive, in their
affemblies. .Thefe affemblies, when legally convoked, were denominated *Comitia*, and were held
in the *Campus Martius* and other parts of Rome ;
being diftinguifhed into *curiata*, *centuriata*, and
tributa, according to the three grand divifions

* I fay the *Campus Martius*, becaufe it was there
the *Comitia* affembled by centuries ; in the two other
forms, they affembled in the *forum* and other places,
where the *capite cenfi* had as much influence and importance as the principal citizens.

of

of the people into *Curiæ*, *Centuries*, and *Tribes*. The *Comitia curiata* were inftituted by Romulus, the *Centuriata* by Servius, and the *Tributa* by the tribunes of the people. Nothing could pafs into a law, nor could any magiftrate be chofen but in the *Comitia*, and as there was no citizen who was not enrolled in a *Curia*, *Century* or *Tribe*, it follows that no citizen was excluded from giving his vote; fo that the Roman people were truly fovereign both in right and fact.

To make the affembly of the *Comitia* legal, and give their determinations the force of laws, three conditions were requifite. In the firft place it was neceffary that the magiftrate or body convoking them, fhould be invefted with proper authority for fo doing: Secondly, that the affembly fhould occur on the days permitted by law; and thirdly, that the augurs fhould be favourable to their meeting.

The reafon of the firft condition needs no explanation: The fecond is an affair of police; thus it was not permitted the *Comitia* to affemble on market days, when the country people, coming to Rome on bufinefs, would be prevented from tranfacting it. By the third, the Senate kept a fierce and turbulent multitude

6   under

under fome reftraint, and opportunely checked the ardour of the feditious tribunes; the latter, however, found more ways than one to elude the force of this expedient.

But the laws and the election of the chiefs were not the only matters fubmitted to the determination of the *Comitia:* the Roman people having ufurped the moft important functions of government, the fate of Europe might be faid to depend on their affemblies. Hence the variety of objects that came before them, gave occafion for divers alterations in the form of thefe affemblies, according to the nature of thofe objects.

To judge of thefe diverfities, it is fufficient to compare them together. The defign of Romulus in inftituting the *Curiæ*, was to reftrain the Senate by means of the people; and the people by the Senate, while he himfelf maintained his influence equally over both. By this form, therefore, he gave to the people all the authority of number to counterballance that of power and riches, which he left in the hands of the Patricians. But, agreeable to the fpirit of monarchy, he gave more advantage to the Patricians, by the influence of their clients to obtain
tain

tain the majority of votes. This admirable inftitution of patrons and clients, was a mafter-
piece of politics and humanity, without which
the order of Patricians, fo contrary to the fpirit
of the republic, could not have fubfifted. Rome
alone hath the honour of giving to the world
this fine example, of which no abufe is known
to have been made, and which neverthelefs hath
never been adopted by other nations.

This divifion by *Curiæ* having fubfifted under
the kings till the time of Servius, and the reign
of the laft *Tarquin* being accounted illegal, the
regal laws came hence to be generally diftinguifhed by the name of *leges curiatæ.*

Under the republic, the *Curiæ*, always confined to the four city tribes, and comprehending only the populace of Rome, could not arrive either at the honour of fitting in the Senate, which was at the head of the Patricians,
or at that of being Tribunes, which, notwithftanding they were Plebeians, were yet at the
head of the citizens in eafy circumftances. They
fell, therefore, into difcredit, and were reduced to fo contemptible a ftate that their thirty
Lictors affembled to do the whole bufinefs of
the *Cimitia curiata.*

The

The divifion by *centuries*, was fo favourable to ariftocracy, that it is not at firft eafy to comprehend why the Senate did not always carry their point in the *Comitia centuriata*, by which the Confuls, Cenfors, and Prætors were chofen. It is in fact certain that out of the hundred and ninety three centuries, forming the fix claffes of the whole Roman people, the firft clafs containing ninety eight of them, and the votes being reckoned only centuries, this firft clafs alone had more votes than all the others. When the centuries of this clafs, therefore, were found to be unanimous, they proceeded no farther in counting votes ; whatever might be determined by the minority being confidered as the opinion of the mob. So that it might be juftly faid, that in the *Comitia centuriata* matters were carried rather by the greater quantity of money, than the majority of votes.

But this extreme authority was moderated by two caufes. In the firft place, the Tribunes, generally fpeaking, and always a confiderable number of wealthy citizens, being in this clafs of the rich, they counterpoized the credit of the Patricians in the fame clafs. The fecond caufe lay in the manner of voting, which was this ; the centuries, inftead of voting according

to

to order, beginning with the firſt in rank, caſt lots which ſhould proceed firſt to the election. And to this the century whoſe lot it was, proceeded * alone; the other centuries being called upon another day to give their votes according to their rank, when they repeated the ſame election, and uſually confirmed the choice of the former. By this method the preference of rank was ſet aſide, in order to give it according to lot, agreeable to the principles of democracy.

There is another advantage reſulting from this cuſtom; which is that the citizens reſiding in the country had time between the two elections to inform themſelves of the merit of the candidates thus proviſionally nominated; by which means they might be better enabled to give their vote. But under the pretence of expediting affairs, this cuſtom was in time aboliſhed, and the two elections were made the ſame day.

* The century thus preferred by lot was called *præ rogatixa*; becauſe it was the firſt whoſe ſuffrage was demanded; and hence is derived the word *prerogatiue.*

The

The *Comitia by Tribes*, were properly speaking the great council of the Roman people. These were convoked only by the Tribunes; by these also the Tribunes were chosen, and by these the *plebiscita* or laws of the people were passed. The Senators were not only destitute of rank in these assemblies; they had not even the right to be present at them; but, obliged to pay obedience to laws in the enacting of which they had no vote, they were in that respect less free than the lowest citizens. This injustice, however, was very ill understood, and was in itself alone sufficient to invalidate the decrees of a body, whose members were not all admitted to vote. Had all the Patricians assisted at these *Comitia*, as they had a right, in quality of citizens, they could have had no undue influence where every man's vote was equal, even from the lowest of the people to the highest personage of the state.

It is evident, therefore, that, exclusive of the good order that resulted from these several divisions, in collecting the votes of so numerous a people, the form and method of these divisions were not indifferent in themselves; each being productive of effects, adapted to
certain

certain views in regard to which it was preferable to any other.

But without entering into a more circumftantial account of thefe matters, it is plain from what hath been advanced, that the *Comitia tribunata* were the moft favourable to a popular government, and the *Comitia centuriata* to an ariftocracy. With refpect to the *Comitia curia a* of which the populace formed the majority, as they were good for nothing but to favour tyrannical defigns, they remained in this contemptible ftate, into which they were fallen; even the contrivers of fedition themfelves not chufing to employ means, which muft have expofed too openly their defigns. It is very certain that all the majefty of the Roman people was difplayed only in the *Comitia centuriata*, which only were compleat; the *curiata* wanting the ruftic Tribes, and the *tribunata* the Senate and Patricians.

With regard to the method of collecting the votes, it was, among the primitive Romans, fimple as their manners, though ftill lefs fimple than that of Sparta. Every one gave his vote aloud, which the regifter took down in writing; the plurality of votes in each tribe, determined the vote of that tribe, and the plurality of votes in the
tribes

tribes determined the fuffrage of the people. In the fame manner alfo they proceeded with regard to the *Curiæ* and the centuries. This cuftom was a very good one, fo long as integrity prevailed among the citizens, and every one was afhamed to give his public fanction to an unworthy perfon or caufe. But when the people grew corrupt and fold their votes, it became neceffary to make them give their votes more privately, in order to reftrain the purchafers by diftruft, and afford knaves an expedient to avoid being traitors.

I know that Cicero cenfures this alteration, and attributes to it in a great degree the ruin of the republic. But, though I am fenfible of all the weight of Cicero's authority in this cafe, I cannot be of his opinion. I conceive, on the contrary, that the ruin of the ftate would have been accelerated, had the Romans neglected making this alteration. As the regimen of people in health, is not proper for the fick, fo it is abfurd to think of governing a corrupt people by the fame laws as were expedient for them before they were corrupted. There cannot be a ftronger proof of this maxim, than the duration of the republic of Venice, the fhadow of which ftill exifts, folely becaufe its laws are adapted only to bad men.

On

On this change in the manner of voting, tablets were diftributed among the citizens, by means of which they could give their fuffrage without its being known. On this occafion other methods were of courfe made ufe of in collecting votes, fuch as counting the number of voices, comparing it with that of the tablets, &c. Not that thefe methods were fo effectual as to prevent the returning officers * from being often fufpected of partiality : and it is plain in the fequel, by the multiplicity of laws made to prevent bribery and corruption in elections, that they could not effect this point.

Toward the decline of the republic, recourfe was had to very extraordinary expedients, to make up for the infufficiency of the laws. Prodigies were fometimes played off with fuccefs; but this fcheme, though it impofed on the multitude, did not impofe on thofe who influenced them. Sometimes affemblies were called fuddenly, and in great hafte, that the candidates might not have time to create an undue intereft : at others again the whole feffions was fpent in declamation, when it was feen that the people

* Cuftodes, ditibitores, rogatores, fuffragiorum.

were

were biaſſed to take a wrong ſide. At length, however, ambition eluded all theſe precautions, and it is almoſt incredible that, in the midſt of ſo many abuſes, this immenſe people ſtill continued, by virtue of their ancient laws, to elect their magiſtrates, to paſs laws, to judge cauſes, and to expedite both public and private affairs, with as much facility as could have been done in the Senate itſelf.

C H A P. V.

On a Tribunate.

WHEN it is impracticable to eſtabliſh an exact proportion between the component parts of a ſtate, or that inevitable cauſes perpetually operate to change their relations, a particular magiſtracy is inſtituted which, not incorporating with the reſt, replaces every term in its true relation, and conſtitutes in itſelf a due medium either between the prince and the people, between the prince and the ſovereign, or, in caſes of neceſſity, at once between both.

This body, which I ſhall call a *Tribunate*, is the preſerver of the laws and of the legiſlative power.

power. It ferves fometimes to protect the fovereign againft the government, as the tribunes
of the people did at Rome; fometimes to protect the government againft the people, as at
prefent the council of the *ten* do at Venice; and
again at others to maintain an equilibrium both
on the one part and the other, as did the Ephori
at Sparta.

The Tribunate is not a conftitutional part
of the city, and ought not, therefore, to have
any fhare in the legiflative or executive power:
even in this however, its own is much greater:
for being able to do nothing itfelf, it may prevent any thing from being done by others. It
is more facred and revered, as defender of the
laws, than the prince who executes them, or
the fovereign who enacts them. This was very
evident at Rome, when the haughty Patricians,
who always defpifed the people collectively,
were neverthelefs obliged to give place to their
common officers, without command or jurifdiction.

The Tribunate when judicioufly moderated
is the firmeft fupport of a good conftitution;
but if it have ever fo little afcendency of power,
it

7

it fubverts every thing. With regard to its weaknefs it is not natural to it; for, provided it have any exiftence at all, it can never have too little power.

It degenerates into tyranny when it ufurps the executive power, of which it is only the moderator, and when it would interpret the laws which it fhould only protect. The enormous power of the Ephori, which was exercifed without danger, while Sparta retained its purity of manners, ferved only to increafe the corruption of them when once begun. The blood of *Agis* fpilt by thofe tyrants was revenged by his fucceffor: the crime and the punifhment of the Ephori accelerated equally the ruin of that republic; for after the time of Cleomenes Sparta was nothing. The deftruction of the Roman republic was effected in the fame manner: the exceffive power which the Tribunes by degrees ufurped, ferved at length, with the help of the laws made in defence of liberty, as a fecurity to the Emperors who deftroyed it. As for the council of *ten* at Venice; it is a moft fanguinary tribunal, equally horrible to the Patricians and the people, and which is fo far from openly protecting the laws, that it now ferves but fecretly to effect the breach of them.

The

The Tribunate is enfeebled, as well as the government, by increasing the number of its members. When the Roman Tribunes, at firſt two, and afterwards five, had a mind to double their number, the Senate did not oppoſe it; being well aſſured they ſhould be able to make one a curb to another; which was actually the caſe.

The beſt way to prevent the uſurpations of ſo formidable a body, a way that no government hath hitherto adopted, would be to render ſuch a body not permanent, but to regulate the intervals during which it ſhould remain diſſolved. Theſe intervals which ſhould not be ſo great as to give abuſes time to ſtrengthen into cuſtoms, might be fixed by law, in ſuch a manner that it would be eaſy to abridge them, in caſe of neceſſity by extraordinary commiſſion.

This method appears to me, to be attended with no inconvenience; becauſe, as I have already obſerved, the Tribunate making no eſſential part of the conſtitution, may be ſuppreſſed without injury: and it appears to me effectual, becauſe a magiſtrate newly re-eſtabliſhed doth not ſucceed to the power of his predeceſſor, but to that which the law confers on him.

L   C H A P.

CHAP. VI.
Of the Dictature.

THAT inflexibility of the laws, which prevents their yielding to circumstances, may in some cases render them hurtful, and in some critical juncture bring on the ruin of the state. The order and prolixity of forms, take up a length of time, of which the occasion will not always admit. A thousand accidents may happen for which the legiflature hath not provided ; and it is a very neceffary forefight to fee that it is impoffible to provide for every thing.

We fhould not be defirous, therefore, of eftablifhing the laws fo firmly as to fufpend their effects. Even Sparta itfelf fometimes permitted the laws to lie dormant.

Nothing, however, but the certainty of greater danger fhould induce a people to make any alteration in government ; nor fhould the facred power of the laws be ever reftrained unlefs the public fafety is concerned. In fuch uncommon cafes, when the danger is manifeft, the public fafety may be provided for by a particular act, which commits the charge of it to thofe who

are

are moſt worthy. Such a commiſſion may paſs, in two different ways, according to the nature of the danger.

If the caſe require only a greater activity in the government, it ſhould be confined to one or two members; in which caſe it would not be the authority of the laws, but the form of the adminiſtration only that would be changed. But if the danger be of ſuch a nature, that the formality of the laws would prevent a remedy, then a ſupreme chief might be nominated who ſhould ſilence the laws, and ſuſpend for a moment the ſovereign authority. In ſuch a caſe, the general Will cannot be doubted, it being evident that the principal intention of the people muſt be to ſave the ſtate from perdition, By this mode of temporary ſuſpenſion the legiſlative authority is not aboliſhed; the magiſtrate who ſilences it, cannot make it ſpeak, and though he over-rules cannot repreſent it; he may do every thing indeed but make laws.

The firſt method was taken by the Roman Senate, when it charged the conſuls, in a ſacred manner, to provide for the ſafety of the

com-

common-wealth. The fecond took place when
one of the confuls nominated a dictator*; a
cuftom which Rome adopted from the example
of Alba.

In the early times of the republic, the Romans had frequent recourfe to the dictatorfhip,
becaufe the ftate had not then fufficient ftability
to fupport itfelf by the force of its conftitution.
The manners of the people, alfo, rendering
thofe precautions unneceffary, which were taken
in after-times, there was no fear that a dictator
would abufe his authority, or that he would
be tempted to keep it in his hands, beyond
the term. On the contrary, it appeared that
fo great a power was burthenfome to the perfon invefted with it, fo eager were they to refign it; as if it were a difficult and dangerous
poft, to be fuperior to the laws.

Thus it was not the danger of the abufe, but
of the debafement of this fupreme magiftracy,

* This nomination was fecretly made in the night,
as if they were afhamed of the action of placing
any man fo much above the laws.

that

that gave occasion to censure the indiscreet use
of it, in ancient times. For when they came
to prostitute it in the affair of elections and o-
ther matters of mere formality, it was very justly
to be apprehended that it would become less
respectable on pressing occasions ; and that the
people would be apt to look upon an office as
merely titular, which was instituted to assist at
empty ceremonies.

Toward the end of the republic, the Romans, becoming more circumspect, were as
sparing of the dictature, as they had before
been prodigal of it. It was easy to see, however, that their fears were groundless, that the
weakness of the capital was their security against
the internal magistrates ; that a dictator might
in some cases have acted in defence of public liberty, without ever making encroachments on
it; and that the Roman chains were not forged
in Rome itself, but in its armies abroad. The
weak resistance which Marius made to Sylla and
Pompey to Cæsar, shewed plainly how little
the authority from within the city could do
against the power from without.

T

This error led them to commit great blunders. Such for inftance, was their neglecting to appoint a dictator in the affair of Cataline. For, as it engaged only the city, or at moft a province in Italy, a dictator invefted with that unlimited authority which the laws conferred on him, might eafily have diffipated that confpiracy, which was with difficulty fuppreffed by a numerous concurrence of fortunate circumftances; which human prudence had no reafon to expect. Inftead of that, the Senate contented itfelf with committing all its power into the hands of confuls; whence it happened that Cicero, in order to act effectually, was obliged to exceed that power in a capital circumftance; and though the public, in their firft tranfports, approved of his conduct, he was very juftly called to an account afterwards for the blood he had fpilt contrary to the laws; a reproach they could not not have made to a dictator. But the eloquence of the conful carried all before it; and preferring, though a Roman, his own glory to his country, he thought lefs of the moft legal, and certain method of faving the ftate, than the means of fecuring all the honour

of

of fuch a tranfaction to himfelf*. Thus was he very juftly honoured as the deliverer of Rome, and as juftly punifhed as the violator of its laws. For, however honourable was his repeal, it was certainly a matter of favour.

After all, in whatever manner this important commiffion may be conferred, it is of confequence to limit its duration to a fhort term; which fhould on no occafion be prolonged. In thofe conjunctures, when it is neceffary to appoint a dictator, the ftate is prefently faved or deftroyed, which caufes being over, the dictature becomes ufelefs and tyrannical. At Rome, the dictators held their office only for fix months; and the greater part refigned before that term expired. Had the time appointed been longer, it is to be apprehended they would have been tempted to make it longer ftill; as did the *decemvir* whofe office lafted a whole year. The dictator had no more time allotted him than was neceffary to difpatch the bufinefs for which he was appointed; fo that he had not leifure to think of other projects.

* This is what he could not be certain of, in propofing a dictator; not daring to nominate himfelf, and not being affured his colleague would do it.

L 4 　　　 C H A P.

CHAP. VII.

Of the Cenforſhip.

AS the declaration of the general will is made
by the laws, ſo the declaration of the
public judgment is made by their cenſure. The
public opinion is a kind of law, which the
Cenſor puts in execution, in particular caſes,
after the example of the prince.

So far, therefore, is the cenſorial tribunal
from being the arbiter of popular opinions, it
only declares them ; and, whenever it departs
from them, its deciſions are vain and inef-
fectual.

It is uſeleſs to diſtinguiſh the manners of a
nation by the objects of its eſteem; for theſe
depend on the ſame principle, and are neceſſarily confounded together. Among all people
in the world, it is not nature, but opinion,
which determines the choice of their pleaſures.
Correct the prejudices and opinions of men, and
their manners will correct themſelves. We always admire what is beautiful, or what appears
ſo ;

ſo ; but it is in our judgment we are miſtaken ;
it is this judgment then we are to regulate.
Whoever judges of manners, takes upon him
to judge of honour; and whoever judges of
honour, decides from opinion.

The opinions of a people depend on the conſtitution ; though the laws do not govern
manners, it is the legiſlature that gives riſe to
them. As the legiſlature grows feeble, manners
degenerate, but the judgment of the cenſors
will not then effect what the power of the laws
have not before effected.

It follows, hence, that the office of a cenſor
may be uſeful to the preſervation of manners,
but never to their re-eſtabliſhment. Eſtabliſh
cenſors during the vigour of the laws ; when
this is paſt, all is over ; no legal means can be
effectual when the laws have loſt their force.

The cenſor is preſervative of manners, by
preventing the corruption of opinions, by maintaining their morality and propriety by judicious applications, and even ſometimes by ſettling
them when in a fluctuating ſituation. The uſe

L 5   of

of feconds in duels, though carried to the greateft excefs in France, was abolifhed by the following words inferted in one of the kings
edicts; *As to thofe who have the cowardice to call
themfelves feconds.* This judgment, anticipating
that of the public, was effectual and put an end
to that cuftom at once. But when the fame
edicts pronounced it cowardice to fight a duel;
though it is certainly true, yet as it was contrary to the popular opinion, the public laughed at a determination fo contrary to their own.

I have obferved elfewhere * that the public
opinion, being fubjected to no conftraint, there
fhould be no appearance of it in the tribunal
eftablifhed to reprefent it. One cannot too
much admire with what art this fpring of action,
entirely neglected among the moderns, was employed by the Romans, and ftill more effectually
by the Lacedemonians.

A man of bad morals, having made an excellent propofal in the council at Sparta, the

* I do but flightly mention here, what I have
treated more at large in my letter to M. d'Alembert.

Ephori,

Ephori, without taking any notice of it, caufed
the fame propofal to be made by a citizen of
character and virtue. How honourable was
this proceeding to the one, and how difgraceful
to the other; and that without directly praifing
or blaming either! Some drunkards of Samos,
having behaved indecently in the tribunal of the
Ephori, it was the next day permitted, by a
public edict, that the Samians might become
flaves. Would an actual punifhment have been
fo fevere as fuch impunity? When the Spar-
tans had once paffed their judgment on the de-
cency or propriety of any behaviour, all Greece
fubmitted to their opinion.

CHAP. VIII.

Of political Religion.

IN the firft ages of the world, men had no
other kings than gods, nor any other government than what was purely theocratical. It
required a great alteration in their fentiments
and ideas, before they could prevail on themfelves, to look upon a fellow creature as a mafter, and think it went well with them.

L 6

Hence,

Hence, a deity being constantly placed at the head of every political society, it followed that there was as many different gods as people. Two communities, personally strangers to each other, and almost always at variance, could not long acknowlege the same master; nor could two armies, drawn up against each other in battle, obey the same chief. Thus Polytheism became a natural consequence of the division of nations, and thence the want of civil and theological toleration, which are perfectly the same, as will be shewn hereafter.

The notion of the Greeks, in pretending to trace their own gods among those of the Barbarian nations, took its rise evidently from the ambition of being thought the natural sovereigns of those people. In this age, however, we think that a most absurd part of erudition, which relates to the identity of the deities of different nations, and according to which it is supposed that Moloch, Saturn and Chronos were one and the same god; and that the Baal of the Phenicians, the Zeus of the Greeks, and the Jupiter of the Latins were the same deity; as if any thing could be found in common

be-

between chimerical beings bearing different names !

If it be afked why there were no religious wars among the Pagans, when every ftate had thus its peculiar deity and worfhip ? I anfwer, it was plainly for this very reafon, that each ftate having its own peculiar religion as well as government, no diftinction was made between the obedience paid to their gods and that due to their laws.   Thus their political were at the fame time theological wars ; and the departments of their deities were prefcribed by the limits of their refpective nations.   The god of one people had no authority over another people ; nor were thefe Pagan deities jealous of their prerogatives ; but divided the adoration of mankind amicably between them.   Even Mofes himfelf fometimes fpeaks in the fame manner of the god of Ifrael: It is true the Hebrews defpifed the gods of the Canaanites, a people profcribed and devoted to deftruction, whofe poffeffions were given them for an inheritance : but they fpeak with more reverence of the deities of the neighbouring nations whom they were forbidden to attack. *Wilt thou not poffefs that,* fays Jeptha to Sihon, king of the Ammonites,

4

·nites, *which Chemoth thy God giveth thee to poffefs? So whomfoever the Lord our God fhall drive
out from before us, them will we poffefs.* There is
in this paffage, I think, an acknowleged fimili-
tude between the rights of Chemofh, and thofe
of the God of Ifrael.

But when the Jews, being fubjected to the
kings of Babylon, and afterwards to thofe of
Syria, perfifted in refufing to acknowlege any
god but their own, this refufal was efteemed
an act of rebellion againft their conquerer, and
drew upon them thofe perfecutions we read of
in their hiftory, and of which no other example
is extant previous to the eftablifhment of chriftianity *.

The religion of every people being thus exclufively annexed to the laws of the ftate, the
only method of converting nations was to fubdue them ; warriors were the only miffionaries ;
and the obligation of changing their religion
being a law to the vanquifhed, they were firft
to be conquered before they were folicited on

* It is evident that the war of the Phocians, called
an holy war was not a religious war. Its object was
to punifh facrilege, and not to fubdue infidels.

this

this head. So far were men from fighting for the gods, that their gods, like those of Homer, fought in behalf of mankind. Each people demanded the victory from its respective deity, and expressed their gratitude for it by the erection of new altars. The Romans before they besieged any fortress summoned its gods to abandon it; and though it be true they left the people of Tarentum in possession of their angry deities, it is plain they looked upon those gods as subjected and obliged to do homage to their own : They left the vanquished in possession of their religion as they sometimes did in that of their laws ; a wreathe for Jupiter of the Capitol, being often the only tribute they exacted.

At length, the Romans having extended their religion with their empire, and sometimes even adopted the deities of the vanquished, the people of this vast empire found themselves in possession of a multiplicity of gods and religions ; which not differing essentially from each other, Paganism became insensibly one and the same religion throughout the world.

Things were in this state, when Jesus came to establish his spiritual kingdom on earth; a design

I

fign which, neceffarily dividing the theological from the political fyftem, gave rife to thofe in-. teftine divifions which have ever fince continued to embroil the profeffion of Chriftianity. Now this new idea of a kingdom in the other world,. having never entered into the head of the Pa- gans, they regarded the Chriftians as actual rebels, who, under an hypocritical fhew of humility, waited only a proper opportunity to render themfelves independent,. and artfully to. ufurp that authority, which in their weak and infant ftate they pretended to refpect: and this. was undoubtedly the caufe of their being per- fecuted.

What the Pagans were apprehenfive of, alfo, did, in procefs of time, actually come to pafs.. Things put on a new face, and the meek Chri- ftians, as their number increafed, changed their tone, while their invifible kingdom of the other world, became, under a vifible head, the moft. defpotic and tyrannical in this.

As in all countries, however, there were ci- vil governors, and laws, there refulted from this two-fold power a perpetual ftruggle for jurifdiction, which renders a perfect fyftem of do-.

domeftic policy almoft impoffible in Chriftian
ftates ; and prevents us from ever coming to a
determination, whether it be the prince or the
prieft we are bound to obey.

Some nations indeed, even in Europe or its
neighbourhood, have endeavoured to preferve
or re-eftablifh the ancient fyftem, but without
fuccefs ; the fpirit of Chriftianity hath univerfally prevailed. Religious worfhip hath always
remained, or again become independent of the
fovereign, and without any neceffary connection
with the body of the ftate. Mahomet had
very falutary and well-connected views in his
political fyftem, and fo long as his modes of
government fubfifted under the caliphs and their
fucceffors, that government remained perfectly
uniform, and fo far good. But the Arabians
becoming wealthy, learned, polite, indolent
and cowardly, were fubdued by the Barbarians :
then the divifion between the two powers re-
commenced ; and though it be lefs apparent
among the Mahometans than among Chriftians,
it is neverthelefs to be diftinguifhed, particularly in the fect of Ali : there are fome ftates,
alfo, as in Perfia, where this divifion is conftantly perceptible.

Among

Among us, the kings of England are placed at the head of the church, as are alfo the Czars in Ruffia : but by this title they are not fo properly mafters as minifters of the religion of thofe countries : they are not poffeffed of the power to change it, but only to maintain its prefent form. Wherever the Clergy conftitute a collective body *, they will be both mafters and legiflators in their own caufe.   There are therefore two fovereigns in England and Ruffia, as well as elfewhere.

Of all Chriftian authors, Mr. Hobbes was the only one who faw the evil and the remedy, and that hath ventured to propofe the re-union

* It muft be obferved, that it is not fo much the formal affemblies of the clergy, fuch as are held in France, which unite them together in a body, as the communion of their churches. Communion and excommunication form the focial compact of the clergy; a compact by means of which they will always maintain their afcendency over both kings and people. All the priefts that communicate together are fellow-citizens, though they fhould be perfonally as diftant, as the extremities of the world. This invention is a mafter-piece in policy. The Pagan priefts had nothing like it; and therefore never had any clerical body.

of

of the two heads of this eagle, and to reſtore that political union, without which no ſtate or government can be well conſtituted.   But he ought to have ſeen that the prevailing ſpirit of Chriſtianity was incompatible with his ſyſtem, and that the intereſt of the Church would be always too powerful for the ſtate. It was not ſo much that which was really falſe and ſhocking in the writings of this philoſopher, as what was really juſt and true, that rendered him odious *.

I conceive that, by a proper diſplay of hi-ſtorical facts, in this point of view, it would be eaſy to refute the oppoſite ſentiments both of Bayle and Warburton ; the former of which pretends that no religion whatever can be of ſervice to the body politic, and the latter that Chriſtianity is its beſt and firmeſt ſupport.   It might be proved againſt the firſt, that every

* In a letter of Grotius to his brother, dated the 11th of April, 1643, may be ſeen what that great Civilian approved and blamed in his book *de cive.* It is true that Grotius, being indulgent, ſeems inclined to forgive the author, the faults of his book, for the ſake of its merits, the reſt of the world, however, were not ſo candid.

state in the world hath been founded on the basis of religion; aud against the second, that the precepts of Christianity are at the bottom more prejudicial than conducive to the strength of the state.

In order to make myself fully understood, I need only give a little more precision to the vague ideas, generally entertained of political religion.

Religion, considered as it relates to society, which is either general or particular, may be distinguished into two kinds, viz. the religion of the man and that of the citizen. The first, destitute of temples, altars, or rites, confined purely to the internal worship of the supreme Being, and to the performance of the eternal duties of morality, is the pure and simple religion of the gospel; this is genuine theism, and may be called the law of natural divinity. The other, adopted only in one country, whose gods and tutelary saints are hence peculiar to itself, is composed of certain dogmas, rites, and external modes of worship prescribed by the laws of such country; all foreigners being accounted Infidels, Aliens and Barbarians; this
kind

kind of religion extends the duties and privileges of men no farther than to its own altars.
Such were all the religions of primitive ages,
to which may be given the name of the law of
civil or positive divinity.

There is a third kind of religion still more
extraordinary, which dividing society into two
legislatures, two chiefs, and two parties, subjects mankind to contradictory obligations, and
prevents them from being at once devotees and
citizens. Such is the religion of the Lamas,
of the Japanese, and of the Roman Catholics;
which may be denominated the religion of the
priests, and is productive of a sort of mixed
and unsociable obligation, for which we have no
name.

If we examine these three kinds of religion
in a political light, they have all their faults.
The third is so palpably defective that it would
be mere loss of time, to point them out. Whatever contributes to dissolve the social union is
good for nothing: all institutions which set
man in contradiction with himself are of no
use.

The

The second is so far commendable as it unites divine worship with a respect for the laws, and that, making the country the object of the people's adoration, the citizen is taught that to serve the state is to serve its tutelary divinity. This is a species of theocracy, in which there should be no other pontiff than the prince, no other priests than the magistrates. To die, in such a state, for their country, is to suffer martyrdom; to violate the laws is impiety; and to doom a criminal to public execration is to devote him to the anger of the gods.

It is blameable, however, in that, being founded on falsehood and deceit, it leads mankind into error; rendering them credulous and superstitious, it substitutes vain ceremonies instead of the true worship of the deity. It is further blameable, in that, becoming exclusive and tyrannical, it makes people sanguinary and persecuting; so that a nation shall sometimes breathe nothing but murder and massacre, and think, at the same time, they are doing an holy action in cutting the throats of those who worship the gods in a different manner from themselves. This circumstance places such a people

in

in a natural ſtate of war with all others, which
is very unfavourable to their own ſafety.

There remains then only the rational and
manly religion of Chriſtianity ; not however,
as it is profeſſed in modern times, but as it is
diſplayed in the goſpel, which is quite another
thing. According to this holy, ſublime, and
true religion, mankind, being all the children
of the ſame God, acknowlege themſelves to be
brothers, and the ſociety which unites them diſ-
ſolves only in death.

But this religion, having no particular relation to the body politic, leaves the laws in poſ-
ſeſſion only of their own force, without adding
any thing to it ; by which means the firmeſt
bonds of ſuch particular ſociety are of no effect. Add to this, that Chriſtianity is ſo far
from attaching the hearts of the citizens to the
ſtate, that it detaches them from it, as well as
from all worldly objects in general : than which
nothing can be more contrary to the ſpirit of
ſociety.

It is ſaid that a nation of true Chriſtians
would form the moſt perfect ſociety imaginable.
To

To this affertion, however, there is one great objection; and this is, that a fociety of true Chriftians would not be a fociety of men. Nay, I will go fo far as to affirm, that this fuppofed fociety, with all its perfection, would neither be of the greateft ftrength nor duration. In confequence of its being perfect, it would want the ftrongeft ties of connexion; and thus this very circumftance would deftroy it.

Individuals might do their duty, the people might be obedient to the laws, the chiefs might be juft, the magiftrate incorrupt, the foldiery might look upon death with contempt, and there might prevail neither vanity nor luxury, in fuch a ftate. So far all would go well; but let us look farther.

Chriftianity is a fpiritual religion, relative only to celeftial objects: the Chriftian's inheritance, is not of this world. He performs his duty, it is true, but this he does with a profound indifference for the good or ill fuccefs of his endeavours. Provided he hath nothing to reproach himfelf with, it is of little importance to him whether matters go well or ill here below.

low. If the ſtate be in a flouriſhing ſituation, he can hardly venture to rejoice in the public felicity, leſt he ſhould be puffed up with the inordinate pride of his country's glory; if the ſtate decline, he bleſſes the hand of God that humbles his people to the duſt.

It is farther neceſſary to the peace and harmony of ſociety, that all the citizens ſhould be without exception equally good Chriſtians; for, if unhappily there ſhould be one of them ambitious or hypocritical, if there ſhould be found among them a Cataline or a Cromwell, it is certain he would make an eaſy prey of his pious countrymen. Chriſtian charity doth not eaſily permit the thinking evil of one's neighbour. No ſooner ſhould an individual diſcover the art of impoſing on the majority, and be inveſted with ſome portion of public authority, than he would become a dignitary. Chriſtians muſt not ſpeak evil of dignities; thus reſpected, he would thence aſſume power; Chriſtians muſt obey the ſuperior powers. Does the depoſitary of power abuſe it? he becomes the rod by which it pleaſes God to chaſtiſe his children.

M   And

242 A TREATISE ON THE

And, would their confciences permit them to drive out the ufurper, the public tranquillity muft be broken, and violence and blood-fhed fucceed; all this agrees but ill with the meeknefs of true Chriftians; and, after all, what is it to them, whether they are freemen or flaves in this vale of mifery? Their effential concern is to work out their falvation, and obtain happinefs in another world; to effect which, their refignation in this, is held to be their duty.

Should fuch a ftate be forced into a war with any neighbouring power? The citizens might march readily to the combat, without thinking of flight; they might do their duty in the field, but they would have no ardour for victory; being better inftructed to die than to conquer. Of what confequence is it to them, whether they are victors or vanquifhed? Think what advantages an impetuous and fanguine enemy might take of their ftoicifm! draw them out againft a brave and generous people, ardently infpired with the love of glory and their country; fuppofe, for inftance, your truly Chriftian republic againft that of Sparta or of Rome; what would be the confequence? Your

3   de-

devout Chriftians would be beaten, difcomfited
and knocked on the head, before they had time
to look about them ; their only fecurity depend-
ing on the contempt which their enemy might
entertain for them. It was, in my opinion, a
fine oath that was taken by the foldiers of Fa-
bius. They did not make a vow either to die
or conquer ; they fwore they would return con-
querors, and punctually performed their oath.
Chriftian troops could not have made fuch a vow,
they would have been afraid of tempting the
Lord their God.

But I am all this while committing a blunder,
in fpeaking of a Chriftian republic ; one of thefe
terms neceffarily excluding the other. Chriftianity inculcates fervitude and dependence ;
the fpirit of it is too favourable to tyrants, for
them not fometimes to profit by it. True Chriftians are formed for flaves ; they know it, and
never trouble themfelves about confpiracies and
infurrections ; this tranfitory life is of too little
value in their efteem.

Will it be faid, the Chriftians are excellent
foldiers ? I deny it. Produce me your Chri-

M 2   ftian

ſtian troops. For my part, I know of no true
Chriſtian ſoldiers. Do you name thoſe of the
Cruſades ? I anſwer, that, not to call in queſtion
the valour of the Cruſaders, they were very
far from being Chriſtian citizens : they were
the ſoldiers of the prieſt, the citizens of the
church ; they fought for its ſpiritual country,
which ſome how or other, it had converted into
a temporal one. To ſet this matter in the beſt
light, it was a kind of return to Paganiſm ; for
as the goſpel did not eſtabliſh any national religion, an holy war could not poſſibly be carried
on by true Chriſtians,

Under the Pagan emperors, the Chriſtian ſoldiers were brave ; of this all the Chriſtian writers aſſure us, and I believe them ; the motive of their bravery was a ſpirit of honour or
emulation, excited by the Pagan troops. But
when the emperors became Chriſtians, this motive of emulation no longer ſubſiſted ; and when
the Croſs had put the Eagle to flight, the
Roman valour diſappeared.

But, laying aſide political conſiderations, let
us return to the matter of right, and aſcertain
                                            its

its true principles with regard to this important point. The right which the focial compact confers on the fovereign, extending no farther than to public utility *, the fubjeft is not accountable to that fovereign, on account of any opinions he may entertain, that have nothing to do with the community. Now, it is of great importance to a ftate, that every citizen fhould be of a religion that may infpire him with a regard for his duty; but the tenets of that religion are no farther interefling to the community than as they relate to morals, and to the difcharge of thofe obligations, which the profeffor lies under to his fellow citizens. If we

---

* *In a republic*, fays the Marquis d'A. *every one is perfectly at liberty, becaufe no one may injure another.* This is the invariable limit of republican liberty, nor is it poffible to ftate the cafe more precifely. I cannot deny myfelf the pleafure of fometimes quoting this manufcript, though unknown to the public, in order to do honour to the memory of an illuftrious and refpeftable perfonage, who preferved the integrity of the citizen even in the miniftry, and adopted the moft unpright and falutary views in the government of his country.

except

except thefe, the individual may profefs what others he pleafes, without the fovereign's having any right to interfere; for, having no jurifdiction in the other world, it is nothing to the fovereign what becomes of the citizens in a future life, provided they difcharge the duties incumbent on them in the prefent.

There is a profeffion of Faith, therefore, purely political; the articles of which it is in the province of the fovereign to afcertain, not precifely as articles of religion, but as the fentiments due to fociety, without which it is impoffible to be a good citizen or faithful fubject *. Without compelling any one to adopt thefe fentiments, the fovereign may alfo equitably banifh him the fociety; not indeed as impious, but as unfociable, as incapable of having a fincere re-

* Cæfar, in pleading for Cataline, endeavoured to eftablifh the doctrine of the Mortality of the Soul: Cato and Cicero, in anfwer to him, did not enter into a philofophical difcuffion of the argument, but contented themfelves with fhewing that Cæfar had fpoken like a bad citizen, and advanced a dogma pernicious to the ftate. And this was in fact the point only that come before the Senate of Rome, and not a queftion in theology.

gard

gard to juftice, and of facrificing his life, if required, to his duty. Again, fhould any one, after having made a public profeffion of fuch fentiments, betray his difbelief of them by his mifconduct, he may equitably be punifhed with death; having committed the greateft of all crimes, that of belying his heart in the face of the laws.

The tenets of political religion fhould be few and fimple; they fhould be laid down alfo wit precifion, and without explication or comment. The exiftence of a powerful, intelligent, beneficent, prefcient and provident Deity; a future ftate; the reward of the virtuous and the punifhment of the wicked; the facred nature of the focial contract, and of the laws; thefe fhould be its pofitive tenets. As to thofe of a negative kind I would confine myfelf folely to one, by forbidding perfecution.

Thofe who affect to make a diftinction between civil and religious toleration, are, in my opinion miftaken. It is impoffible to live cordially in peace with thofe whom we firmly believe devoted to damnation : to love them would be to hate the Deity for punifhing them, it is therefore abfolutely neceffary for us either to

per-

perfecute or to convert them. Wherever the spirit of religious perfecution subsists, it is impossible it should not have some effect on the civil police, in which cafe, the sovereign is no longer sovereign even in a secular view; the priests become the real masters, and kings only their officers.

In modern governments, where it is impossible to support an exclusive national religion, it is requisite to tolerate all such, as breathe the spirit of toleration toward others, provided their tenets are not contradictory to the duty of a good citizen. But whosoever should presume to say, *There is no salvation out of the pale of our church*, ought to be banished the state; unless indeed the state be an ecclesiastical one, and the prince a pontiff. Such a dogma is of use only in a theocratical government; in every other it is destructive. The reason which it is said Henry IV. gave, for embracing the Roman Catholic religion, ought to have made an honest man reject it, and more particularly a prince capable of reasoning on the subject.

C H A P.

CHAP. IX.

The Conclusion.

HAVING thus ſtated the true principles of politic law, and endeavoured to fix the ſtate on its proper baſis, it remains to ſhew in what manner it is ſupported by external relations.

Under this head would be comprehended, the laws of nations and commerce, the laws of war and conqueſt, leagues, negotiations, treaties, &c. But theſe preſent a new proſpect, too vaſt and extenſive for ſo ſhort a ſight as mine; which ſhould be confined to objects leſs diſtant and more adapted to my limited capacity.

F I N I S.

In the Prefs, and fpeedily will be publifhed,

THE

MISCELLANEOUS WORKS

OF

Mr. J. J. ROUSSEAU.

Alfo,

A NEW EDITION,

Revifed and Corrected from the Author's laft
corrected Copy. In 4 Volumes.

E L O I S A:

OR, A

Series of Original Letters between two Lovers.

By Mr. J. J. ROUSSEAU.